Lesley Irene Shore, PhD

Tending Inne
The Heali
of Feminist Psyc...herapy

" **L** esley Shore's book, *Tending Inner Gardens,* is a beautiful meditation on the parallel between feminist psychotherapy and gardening. It will be enjoyed greatly by psychotherapists just starting out, because it describes in some detail how experience and continuing education transform and season a therapist and, in turn, how an experienced therapist transforms the doctrinaire teachings she has learned into tools to nurture the flowers in her garden — her patients."

Aline Zoldbrod, PhD
Psychologist in Private Practice;
Author, *Men, Women, and Infertility: Intervention and Treatment Strategies*

More pre-publication
REVIEWS, COMMENTARIES, EVALUATIONS . . .

"**L**esley Shore gives us an intimate and dynamic understanding of how she works and thinks, both as a gardener tending nature's soil and as a therapist tending the inner soil of another product of nature–women and men. Reflecting her feminism, Dr. Shore utilizes her feelings and life experiences to bring depth to her work. After describing her early personal and professional experiences, Dr. Shore then proceeds on to Harmony Farm, where she currently lives and where the themes of this book find inspiration. The atmosphere, the constantly changing seasons, and the visual sensations of Harmony Farm are beautifully detailed. Of particular significance are the chapters on language and the use of the metaphor in psychotherapy to grasp the emotional history of a person as well as her/his current concerns. . . . Readers will find the book engrossing."

Conalee Levine-Shneidman, PhD
Psychoanalyst in Private Practice,
New York City; Author,
Too Smart for Her Own Good?

"*Tending Inner Gardens* is a loving and naturalistic description of psychotherapy, helping both client and therapist to value the variety of seasons in the healing process. With a keen gardener's eye, Dr. Shore tills a rich soil of Jungian concepts, David Grove's linguistic technique for fertilizing the therapeutic metaphor, and feminine time and space–with an illustrative case history.

Most therapists will treasure her exposition on 'Mud Season,' the fine art of composting in psychotherapy, and her image of every human being as needing to pay attention both to their outward stem (reaching for the sun) and their inward roots (gathering nourishment from the contextual ground). A wise and soothing book, *Tending Inner Gardens* gives credence to the notion of psychotherapy as a spiritual journey for both client and therapist."

Priscilla Cogan, PhD
Clinical Psychologist
in Private Practice,
Mechanicsville, Maryland

The Harrington Park Press
An Imprint of The Haworth Press, Inc.

Tending Inner Gardens
The Healing Art
of Feminist Psychotherapy

HAWORTH Innovations in Feminist Studies
Esther Rothblum, PhD and Ellen Cole, PhD
Senior Co-Editors

Tending Inner Gardens
The Healing Art of Feminist Psychotherapy

Lesley Irene Shore, PhD

Harrington Park Press
An Imprint of The Haworth Press, Inc.
New York • London • Norwood (Australia)

Published by

Harrington Park Press, an imprint of The Haworth Press, Inc., 10 Alice Street, Binghamton, NY 13904-1580

Library of Congress Cataloging-in-Publication Data

Shore, Lesley Irene.
    Tending inner gardens : the healing art of feminist psychotherapy / Lesley Irene Shore.
       p.   cm.
    Includes bibliographical references and index.
    ISBN 1-56023-856-9 (acid free paper.)
    1. Feminist therapy–Philosophy. 2. Psychotherapy–Philosophy.
I. Title
RC489.F45S53   1994
616.89′14′01–dc20   93-36036
                                                                 CIP

To
the people who
planted my garden,
protected it, nurtured it,
and ensured it would thrive:

Hanna Fischmann Shore
and
Felix Francis Shore

ABOUT THE AUTHOR

Lesley Irene Shore, PhD, is a psychologist with over 25 years of varied experience working in counseling centers, hospitals, and a clinic. She has held academic appointments at Harvard Medical School and the Massachusetts School for Professional Psychology. The author of *Healing the Feminine: Reclaiming Woman's Voice*, she now practices on Harmony Farm in Medfield, Massachusetts. Dr. Shore is a member of the American Psychological Association (Division 35, Psychology of Women) and the Association for Women in Psychology and is a Fellow in the Massachusetts Psychological Association.

CONTENTS

Seasons

Acknowledgements

Many people contributed to the compost that nourished this work – all my teachers, supervisors, colleagues, family members, friends, and acquaintances. Some planted seeds; others encouraged my growth. There are too many to list, but I am indebted to you all.

Generous souls read my manuscript during various stages of its development. I am grateful to Priscilla Cogan, Sharon Bard, Maida Greenberg, Geri Reinhardt, Hanna Shore, Kathleen Spivack, and Tina Van De Water for the hours they each spent trudging through rough terrain. These people helped with many garden chores, especially weeding, pruning and extra fertilizing.

I am fortunate to have a good friend, Priscilla Cogan, who also writes between psychotherapy appointments. Our walks on the beach and chats on the phone enrich my work in both professions. Her incisive editorial comments, punctuated by puns and exhortations, challenge my writing.

I am thankful that the Senior Editors of Haworth Innovations in Feminist Studies, Ellen Cole and Esther Shapiro, believed that this work should be published. Ellen Cole treated me with dignity and respect, and kept me apprised as to the status of my manuscript throughout the review process – a consideration frequently lacking in the publishing industry. Her gracious attitude typified my experiences with the people of The Haworth Press.

My manuscript became a book under the capable direction of Bill Cohen, Publisher, and Bill Palmer, Managing Editor. I thank the Copyeditor, Lisa Levine, for her meticulous attention to detail. Lisa McGowan, Production Editor, sorted through all my corrections of their corrections with infinite patience and refreshing good humor. Patricia Brown, Assistant Editor, and Peg Marr, Proofreader, helped ensure that this book is as free of errors as possible. Others who contributed their fine skills include: Laura Frederick and Sandra Ceplo, Editorial Assistants, and Joan Drake, Administrative Assistant.

My husband, Bill Tragakis, once said that my second book would be easier to write than my first. He was right. But I never could have written it without his loving support.

Last, but certainly not least, I am indebted to my clients–all the people who trusted me with their struggles, their shame, and their secrets. They continually teach me about the process of change. And while I would have liked to specifically thank those who are mentioned in this book, psychotherapy is a private matter and I have protected their identities by giving them pseudonyms.

Harmony Farm
Medfield, Massachusetts

Introduction

Although I consider myself a feminist, I tend to avoid using this frequently misunderstood word. In our polarized world, feminism conjures up images of angry women bent on revenge. Women have every right to be angry, but feminism has nothing to do with revenge. Feminism is committed to creating equality between the sexes, and restoring balance between masculine and feminine.

The field of psychotherapy has been overly influenced by masculine models. Feminist therapists aim to correct this imbalance by offering alternate ways of thinking about therapy. Attempting to compensate for inequities, their approaches value traditionally feminine traits such as intuition, empathy, connection, and caring.

I wrote this book because I wanted to share my personal vision of psychotherapy – a way of thinking about therapy that does not reject previous formulations, but includes them in a broader panorama. I believe we need a new model, a truly feminist model, one that values both the masculine AND feminine perspectives.

This book presents a model of psychotherapy that integrates masculine and feminine constructs within a naturalistic framework. It recognizes that masculine and feminine are balanced in nature, and that psychotherapy relies on nature's growing and healing processes. Nature's rhythms, cycles, and balancing processes are our healing resources!

The first section of this book, *Nature*, lays the foundation for a natural model of psychotherapy. It describes nature's seasonal cycle and introduces the idea that therapists are gardeners who work with nature's processes to facilitate growth.

The next section discusses the *Tools* of psychotherapy, its techniques. While my approach is rooted in the psychoanalytic method, I have incorporated other techniques into my work. I describe some of these tools, and pay particular attention to language because many therapists have not been trained to use language skillfully.

The techniques I cover are not new, nor do they comprise an exhaustive list of the many methods currently available if one is open to using tools from different models such as the cognitive, behavioral, family systems, and psychoanalytic formulations. In my opinion, psychotherapy isn't a technique. It's a process. Any technique can be useful if it offers a way of facilitating growth and helping people heal their inner wounds.

Seasons, the last section, is the heart of this book. It proposes that nature's seasonal cycle is a model for the psychotherapy process. These chapters discuss practical aspects of therapy while following one client's progress through the seasons of her therapy.

A natural model of psychotherapy transcends the artificial dichotomies currently characterizing much psychological thought. This method works with opposites – masculine and feminine processes that are linear as well as circular, active as well as passive, moving inward as well as outward. These opposites complement each other, enabling people to recover from emotional injuries and find balance as whole human beings.

I hope that this book leaves you with an increased appreciation for the process – of psychotherapy – of nature – of life.

Nature

Models

When I went to college, most of my classmates were male. This imbalance was even more pronounced among the faculty, in which females were few and far between. The textbooks we read were generally written by males. I struggled with feelings of inadequacy and worried about whether I'd be able to succeed, but never considered the possibility that these feelings could be societally induced.

Despite feelings of insecurity, I studied diligently and completed my coursework in less than four years. But when I went to the placement office looking for a job, the person who interviewed me asked if I could type and then suggested that I apply for a secretarial position. Instead, I went to graduate school.

After obtaining a Master's degree, I finally qualified for my first professional position, on the staff of a college counseling center. Although that college was coed, prior to my arrival all the therapists had been male. Need I mention the sex of the secretaries?

Two males, both psychoanalytically trained, supervised my work. They discouraged my inclination to connect with clients. And when my feelings of inadequacy inadvertently rose to the surface, affecting my work, they referred me to a therapist – a male analyst.

Recognizing that I needed further training, I entered a doctoral program in Counseling Psychology. Although most of the professors were male, fortunately I signed up for a practicum that happened to be taught by a woman, Dr. Conalee Levine-Shneidman. Connie, as she invited us to call her, became my first female supervisor. She encouraged me to find my own way as a therapist, letting me know that caring for clients could be helpful to them – as long as I kept my issues out of their therapy. And as she fostered my development by helping me trust my own perceptions, she inadvertently also facilitated my growth as a female therapist. I still model myself after her.

In contrast to me, Connie impressed me as a unique person, a whole human being. I sought her out in a variety of ways, approaching her with personal questions about how she balanced the many aspects of her life – her roles as wife, mother, professional woman, and therapist. By answering my questions honestly, Connie helped me begin working through my own issues about being a professional woman. She let me know that there are never simple solutions to complicated issues. And, most importantly, she gave me my first taste of a collaborative relationship with someone in authority.

Connie was ahead of her time, a liberated woman. As I moved on with my career, most of my teachers and supervisors continued to be men. Because I was eager to learn how to be helpful to others, I emulated these more experienced professionals. I didn't question their techniques or their authority.

When people like Betty Friedan and Simone de Beauvoir started raising their voices, demanding to be heard, they struck chords in many women, including myself, by putting words to feelings I'd been trying to ignore. I finally acknowledged feeling angry about the many abuses inflicted on women, and came to believe that men should be held responsible for their actions. However, I also felt uncomfortable about blaming men for the cultural bias against women. Although I couldn't yet articulate the larger issues involved, I sensed there was an underlying dynamic being played out between men and women.

The women's movement gathered momentum, promoting equality between the sexes. And while many gains were made, too many underlying issues remained the same. Men continued subjugating women. And women complained of feeling inadequate, inferior, and not good enough.

I, too, struggled with feelings of insecurity, not only in my personal life, but also in the professional arena. After completing my course work, I worked in a variety of hospitals and an outpatient clinic. The populations differed, but the environments were similar: for regardless of the institution, I often felt demeaned and minimized. As a psychologist in medical settings where doctors are granted more privileges – and accorded respect – regardless of their level of expertise, I was relegated to second-class citizenship. In addition, some male colleagues had difficulty treating me, a woman, as a fellow professional; they used a variety of tactics to put me down. And, making a bad situation even more abusive, one superior took advantage of his position by trying to sexualize our relationship.

Despite these difficulties, I grew more adept as a therapist by attending seminars, heeding supervisors' advice, and, most of all, learning from clients. However, I often felt like a fraud, for what I did in my office wasn't necessarily thought out in advance. Although I didn't plan interventions or use specific techniques according to well-formulated plans, there were usually good reasons why I acted as I did. Instead of systematically analyzing clients' difficulties and acting according to the diagnostic category, I listened carefully to them and responded to my sense of what would be most helpful at the time.

While my knowledge definitely influenced how I behaved with clients, I also knew that what I said at any given time in a particular session was often intuitive, based on a feeling of what needed to be said right then. This process seemed different from the way most of my colleagues and supervisors spoke of their work. They tended to talk about psychotherapy in intellectual terms; the intuitive aspects of the work were frequently overlooked.

After working primarily with adolescents and their parents, usually their mothers, I moved into an adult-oriented private practice where many of my clients were women. They suffered from a variety of symptoms. Some were depressed; others, anxious. Many had eating disorders. As I continued working with women, I started hearing similar themes, regardless of their presenting problems. In addition to focusing on other people while demeaning themselves, practically all the women had negative feelings about their bodies. In thinking about their difficulties, I realized that my female clients weren't grounded in their selves. They were dissociated from essential parts of themselves.

I also worked with men. Listening to them, I initially heard different issues, for they were generally more confident, more sure of their selves. Unlike the women, they tended to speak in intellectual terms. They had denounced their softer, feeling, more feminine sides.

Although it appeared that men and women struggle with difficulties unique to their sex, I started seeing a deeper, societal dynamic at play. The intrapsychic dynamics differ for men and women, but everyone has issues with the feminine. Regardless of gender, the feminine is suppressed, oppressed, abused (Shore 1992d).

The theoretical constructs of "masculine" and "feminine" are frequently confused with gender. Even some ardent feminists fall into society's trap of identifying male with masculine and female with feminine. However, our society isn't just biased against women. The issue is with the feminine.

We live in an over-masculinized world. It is a world created in His image, ruled over by a male God with a masculine view of the universe, structured according to power. This world not only splits masculine from feminine and segregates these qualities according to gender, it also values the masculine at the expense of the feminine.

Our culture esteems mental processes such as logic and reason, usually categorized as masculine, while distrusting feelings, which are generally associated with the feminine. As it also emphasizes the importance of objectivity, separation, and disconnection, the scientific method has become the only respected means for gathering information. We discount intuition – the more feminine, bodily way of knowing.

Society's glorification of the masculine and suppression of the feminine affects every aspect of our lives. It forms the basis of perception, structures our psyches, and influences our relationships. Our model of healing is also biased toward the masculine.

The role of the healer has always been associated with the sacred. As we look to healers to intercede, to influence forces of life and death, it is no wonder that their role has been linked to the divine. And when the divine had a feminine face, our model of healing emphasized feminine qualities.

A feminine healing tradition existed long before the advent of the scientific method (Campbell, 1980; Stone, 1976; Walker, 1983). This ancient tradition has come to be known as the wise woman tradition. It is one we know very little about, but have begun piecing together a story of women's knowledge that dates back to very early times, to thousands of years ago, before Christ, before a male God. It was a time when nature and the feminine were worshipped, when women were identified with life forces – with creativity, giving birth, and finding food (Gimbutas, 1982, 1989). Women were seen as close to nature, in touch with the mysterious rhythms of life and death.

During these early times, healing involved the spirit and tasks of motherhood. In this nurturing model of healing, the traditional lore of women contained wisdom based on centuries of observation and experience. Wise women studied nature and learned how to use this resource for healing. They used all their senses, including intuition, in gathering information. Their knowledge was handed down through generations, from one person to another, from one wise woman to the next. And when wise women administered herbal remedies, they remained with the ill person throughout the healing process, watching them, touching them, connecting with them in every possible way.

The world view gradually changed to one that worshipped a transcendent, heavenly father God. Heaven (mind) and earth (body) were split into a hierarchy, and the earth was associated with more lowly, feminine qualities. Witch hunts followed in the wake of these changes as the feminine model of healing was overpowered, supplanted by a masculine model (Ehrenreich & English, 1979).

The scientific method is a masculine model. It is a systematic rather than intuitive approach that couples impartial observation and objectivity with manipulation and control of variables. Our medical model is rooted in this mechanistic tradition.

The medical model is a hierarchical, distancing model. Patients are treated. After their problems are analyzed, often with the help of sophisticated machines, they are given substances designed to attack and defeat the purported cause of their difficulties. Sometimes the physician applies additional power and skill; he operates on the patient.

In this model, patients generally aren't credited with participation in the healing process. Patients are expected to comply with doctors' orders by taking prescribed pills at appointed times. Usually the pill and the surgeon's skill are accorded the power to heal – unless these efforts fail. Then the patient is blamed.

Despite psychology's philosophical roots – *psyche* originally meant soul – it hasn't escaped domination by the masculine. The case study approach, which harkens back to wise women's ways, has fallen into disrepute. In order for research to yield significant information, it must be methodologically sound, impartially executed by a detached investigator, and evaluated by statistical analysis.

Psychotherapy not only originated within the medical model, it has now been invaded by managed care. Therapists have traditionally been expected to maintain a distant, uninvolved, stance – imitating the purportedly sterile environments of the petri dish and operating room. In recent developments, therapists are also expected to simulate assembly line efficiency, for behavior must be shaped, modified, in ten sessions or less. Care is now managed – meted out according to the diagnostic axes of DSM formulae.

Most psychotherapists agree that although some symptoms readily resolve, deeply rooted difficulties can require lengthy exploration. Nevertheless, many therapists passively acquiesce and struggle to comply with managed care by offering palliative solutions to complicated processes. In doing so, we inadvertently contribute to the increased masculinization, and mechanization, of psychotherapy.

While our world might have been initially biased toward the feminine, it is currently tilted in a masculine direction. However, systems generally move toward balance; imbalance promotes change. It has taken a long time, but the pendulum has started swinging in the opposite direction – toward the feminine.

Our world view is shifting. Some people are questioning the concept of an all-seeing powerful God and resurrecting ancient Goddess-worshipping rituals. Ecologically minded people are recognizing that by focusing attention solely on the heavens, we've neglected our earth. Physicians such as Bernie Siegal (1986) and Dean Ornish (1990) are writing about love and compassion. Women are refusing to be victimized by agents of the masculine. And men are trying to listen to feelings. The feminine has been raising her voice, demanding to be heard.

Whenever pendulums move away from one side of a polarity, there's always the danger they'll shift too far in the opposite direction. Instead of replacing masculine models with feminine ones, we need models that value both the feminine and the masculine. Masculine and feminine balance each other. Together they create a whole.

My supervisor, Connie, struck me as a whole person because,

due to her unique background, she embodied the masculine as well as the feminine. Her work reflected this balance. While she cared deeply for her clients, and wasn't afraid to become involved, she managed to maintain a professional stance. No wonder I've modelled myself after her.

I suspect that talented therapists, both male and female, have always valued the feminine as well as the masculine, trusted their intuition as well as their reason, and listened to their bodies as well as their minds. And good clinicians, whether physicians or wise women, learn from their clients as well as research documented by others. In order to articulate these processes, we need a model of healing that's capable of incorporating the masculine as well as the feminine. Then we can pass this information from one person to another, and from one generation to the next.

Gardening

I am a traditionally trained psychologist. I went to the proper schools, took the relevant courses, learned the theories, and followed professorial advice. After being trained by people respected in my professional circle, I spent over 20 years working within various social institutions, from college counseling centers to hospitals to outpatient clinics. During this time I not only developed into an experienced therapist, I also began supervising others. There are those who would say I had a successful career, for I was given impressive titles and responsibilities. Yet with all these credentials, my own growth had been stunted. Enmeshed in our overly masculine, mechanistic world – a world that values mind over body – I failed to recognize that many current psychotherapy practices perpetuate societal imbalances. By connecting me with nature, gardening gave me the missing tools for helping people become whole human beings.

Although I was drawn to nature and used to think of myself as connecting with her, I didn't realize how separated I was from her, how much I had relegated nature to the background of life. When I was on ski slopes, every inch of fresh snow was a welcome delight. Standing on top of a mountain, surrounded by white peaks and blue skies, I felt overwhelmed by nature's magnificence. Yet, once I returned home the snow became an impediment, preventing me from getting to work on time, forcing me to deal with a driveway filled with natural white fluff. In retrospect, I felt separate from nature.

I was like most people, for our society is built on control, order, and predictability. As civilization became increasingly mechanized, dominated by the masculine, the feminine was relegated outside, to nature's domain. Society is now identified with the masculine, while nature is identified with the feminine.

Nature has been set up as the counterpoint of culture – the repository of the irrational, the unpredictable, the feminine. We have not only lost our ties with Mother Earth and Father Sky, but "She" became the enemy. As issues of power and control pervade our attitude toward nature, we abuse "Her." We rape land, defoliate forests, and pollute the air, the ocean, the earth (Griffin, 1978; Merchant, 1980; Plant, 1989).

My attitude toward nature began changing when my husband and I moved our family from a suburban, cosmopolitan area to a more rural setting. We had a vague fantasy of living on a farm, and anticipated that this move would have a beneficial effect on everyone in the family. Little did we realize that the effects would reverberate through every aspect of our lives.

The land started calling to me even before we settled into the house. I dreamed of digging in soil, planting daffodils and lilacs, and being surrounded by flowers. As soon as possible, a shovel was found to answer this call and help implement my vision. While I was busy bending my back developing herb gardens, strawberry beds, and wildflower patches, my husband labored in the field, creating row after row of vegetable growing space.

Our connection with the land deepened. And, as this happened, our concerns about health and nutrition branched into conservation, ecology, and sustainable agriculture. Our commitment to growing healthy wholesome food for feeding our family gradually developed into a lifestyle of living in harmony with nature, and we named our home Harmony Farm.

Gardening was an important part of this lifestyle. It linked the rhythms of our life with nature's cycles. For the first time in my life, I not only paid attention to the seasons, I also began living more in tune with my own body and the cycles of our Earth.

Even though we live in climate-controlled homes, our bodies tune into the rhythms of the area. As I've primarily lived in the Northeast, where we move through four distinct seasons, my body always cycled with these seasons, craving cool, fresh fruits and vegetables during summer, and hungering for warm soups and stews during winter. Prior to our move, I never paid much attention to these cycles. I even tended to give my houseplants the same supply of water all year round, carrying on as if each week was like the one before.

Gardening on Harmony Farm connected me with a larger universe – the cycles of earth, moon, and sun. Our lifestyle now follows the rhythm of these cycles. By attending to information gathered through our senses, we keep time with the day and stay in tune with the seasons.

I'm fortunate to live in a house with large expanses of glass that keep us visually linked to nature's happenings. If we don't hear the rooster's crow welcoming the morning sun, we wake up to light brightening our room, inviting us out of bed. And even though electric lights keep our bodies alert after the sun disappears into the horizon, we try to lay our heads on pillows as soon afterward as possible.

Before living on Harmony Farm I expected my body to keep a similar schedule regardless of seasonal variations in the length of daylight. Now I no longer bemoan summer days of waking up fully alert at the crack of dawn, or winter nights of sleeping through the clock's buzzing reminder of chores to be done and appointments to keep. On Harmony Farm we recognize these shifts as natural. When we listen to our bodies, we tend to sleep more during winter and less in summer.

As the earth journeys around the sun, moving from winter to spring, through summer, and into fall, nature's green thread weaves its way through the seasons of the year. Winter begins weaving into spring when touches of green appear on the horizon. Tree trunks change color as their sap starts to flow. Then bulbs push their heads above ground, testing the air to see if it's safe to appear. The air vibrates with excitement and expectation. Soon green appears everywhere, elongating and expanding, bursting forth into stem, leaf, and plant. Buds on trees swell, filling with green. Elastic movement resounds with green – a symphony of creation. The greening of spring signals birth and rebirth.

After spending winter sitting in front of the fireplace, leafing through seed catalogues and dreaming of warm summer days, we too come to life after winter's rest. We poke our noses outdoors and breathe the fresh spring air. Spring is a time of boundless energy, of restless feverish activity bursting forth. We call it spring fever – a time of rebirth, reawakening, falling in love with life. Spring is a busy time of digging, weeding, and sowing seed as we join hands with nature and go about planting our food for the year. It's time to send our roots into the earth and feel renewed, replenished. The annual spring cleaning ritual is a welcome event.

The rites of spring begin bearing fruit in summer as Mother Nature slows her pace and focuses on ripening. She weaves the warmth of summer sun with the sustenance of earth, creating a seasonal palette of fresh ripe fruit. Summer is our barefooted, brown-back time of gathering and harvesting the fruit of her labor, food that will nourish us through long winter months. It's time to be outside, soaking in the warmth of the sun.

As the heat of summer takes its toll, nature increasingly slows her pace. She weaves her way through fall, dropping colors along the way, concentrating her energy on preparing to sleep. She is eager to begin to rest, to lay her head upon a mossy cushion and begin dreaming the dreams of winter. Birds fly south to warmer climates, along with some of our friends and relatives.

Animals that remain in cooler regions retreat beneath the earth where their body rhythms slow down. We behave like squirrels, stocking supplies by stuffing the freezer and filling the larder. We begin retreating within.

Winter is the time to hibernate, to rest and repair. Snowflakes drift down outside our window, blanketing the ground, keeping green warm during her winter sleep. Though nature may be taking a well-deserved rest, her presence continues to be felt throughout our home. There are green beans in the freezer; carrots, potatoes, and beets in the cold storage room. All are ready and waiting to be used in the pot atop the wood stove. Herbs that have been dried to preserve nature's green essence hang from rafters, ready to lend their aroma and taste to a warming tea. Over the years, nature has taught me about the herbs so that summer's harvest can nurture and heal, even during winter.

My body tells me to rest during early winter, to hibernate along with my fellow creatures of nature. And while I may call myself "seasonally depressed," I attend to my body's signals. As I curl up beside the fire, winter is the time to read a good book, to reminisce, or reflect. The fire burning in the hearth is a gift from nature, for she carefully nurtured the wood and watched its growth. We will dutifully return the ashes to her, putting them back in the earth when the warm air of spring threads down, softening the ground, preparing for spring.

After living on Harmony Farm for a couple of years, I began feeling more connected with myself – more complete, whole, and centered. While I had difficulty describing the shifts taking place inside me, I sensed I was blossoming and that something important had happened. I wanted my clients to partake of the fruit.

Attributing my changes to the place rather than a process, I decided to expose all my clients to Harmony Farm's healing influence. I resigned from my position at an outpatient clinic and expanded my private practice on Harmony Farm. I was on my own.

At first I was lonely. I missed the collegial connections, the sharing of cases, and the opportunities for quick consultations at the coffeepot. Then I started appreciating the quiet, the solitude, the space to explore on my own and find my own way of doing therapy.

My perspective shifted when I began working on my own. I saw things differently, for I had never realized how much my thinking had been limited by society's framework. When my office was less connected with that world, closer to nature, I listened to clients in new ways. And between sessions I gardened.

As I became less enmeshed in social institutions, the walls between garden and office inadvertently crumbled. Before I realized what was happening, I started using my gardening tools in my office. Just as in the garden, I used all of my senses, including intuition, for gathering information. And I gradually learned about a growing and healing process that was more encompassing and powerful than any of the psychotherapy techniques I'd previously struggled to emulate.

The garden was my teacher. And there was much to learn about working with nature, using her processes. Like our attitude toward weather, many people approach gardening expecting to exercise control over the process. To make sure that their efforts pay off, they attack bugs with pesticides, kill weeds with herbicides, and pour soil amendments into the earth. These practices are not only hazardous to our health, they also promote imbalances in nature which, over time, tend to increase (rather than decrease) soil and pest problems. And while organic gardening books and workshops taught me many beneficial practices, the garden gave me a most important lesson for someone who has grown up in our society. The lesson concerns control, and it's an annual event in our garden.

After anxiously awaiting the arrival of spring, the soil softens, we sow some seed, and we eagerly watch for signs of growth. Green appears, and a plant forms. We pamper it, water it, nurture it. And then, sometimes, it suddenly disappears, head decapitated, arms amputated. Other plants escape unscathed, continuing to grow, blossom, and begin bearing fruit. But then, while our backs are momentarily turned, the fruit mysteriously vanishes. Whole crops have been demolished. Sometimes we're lucky and find a few remaining beanstalks, ears of corn, or tomatoes.

This damage is the handiwork of clandestine visitors. Local woodchucks, rabbits, deer, raccoons, and other wild creatures seem to think that we tend broccoli and beans especially for them. We try to be philosophical and accept the inevitability of sharing our life with all of nature, including these creatures from the wild. We remind ourselves that "these experiences are part of living a natural life. We don't own the garden – merely participate in the process." Yet we're discouraged, frustrated, and angry.

After all our work and eager anticipation, it's hard to accept losses, be prepared to share, and possibly lose it all. Learning to accept loss is a lifelong lesson – a lesson in being able to give as well as to receive, to give up as well as to get. Loss is part of life.

Our garden continues teaching us about giving up control. We now purposely plant extra – some for them and some for us. And while we hope there will be plenty for all, we can never be sure. There are always surprises.

Gardening is an antidote for the ills of living in a mechanistic world. After years of living in a world dominated by the masculine, important aspects of myself had been closed off from experience, banished from awareness, lost. By connecting me with nature, gardening gave these stunted, neglected, undeveloped parts of my self an opportunity to develop. As I sent roots deep into the soil, starved parts of myself were nourished, and I unearthed the wise woman within me. Nature tended my inner garden.

Gardening taught me something that my other education had neglected. It connected me with nature's growing and healing processes. As I participated in these fundamental processes, felt them inside, buried senses came alive and my therapy changed. It became less analytic, more balanced between mind and body. I discovered a model of psychotherapy that taps into nature's healing resources.

The tools of psychotherapy are similar to those of gardening. Fertilizing and weeding, raking and hoeing, digging and mulching can't make people grow, but they can assist nature's growing and healing processes. These processes follow a seasonal cycle. By tending inner gardens we help people nourish the soil within their selves and grow into whole human beings.

Developing

We are born with many seeds. While each seed is full of potential – ready to develop and waiting to unfold – only some of these seeds will be able to germinate. Each seed must wait for the specific conditions that are conducive to its particular growth.

My "psychologist seed" lay dormant for many years. When I went to college, it found the right time and place and began to germinate. As my concern for people, especially their emotional lives, thrived within psychology's fertile soil, I decided to major in the field. Psychology felt right.

The university environment can support the growth of many seeds. While my interest in psychology continued to develop, I was also pulled toward the Oriental humanities, attracted to something that was there, something that seemed missing elsewhere. While Oriental philosophy recognizes differences, it also acknowledges the complementarity of opposites, the underlying connections between seemingly disparate phenomena. It recognizes balance, the balance created through the interplay of opposites – between disconnection and connection, between masculine and feminine. This balance is seen as forming a whole, a circle divided into yin and yang, complementary interacting opposites. In contrast to the mechanistic soil of western psychology, Oriental philosophy is more naturalistic and holistic.

Western psychology and Oriental philosophy spoke to different parts of me. While these seeds initially existed side by side, psychology began taking up more and more space as I became increasingly enamored with the goal of becoming a psychologist and wholeheartedly pursued this dream. Cultivating this seed demanded all my attention, all my energy.

My love affair with Oriental philosophy became a fond memory. This holistic orientation was pushed aside, for it wasn't considered compatible with the science of psychology. Instead of connections, communalities, and wholes, I was educated in differences.

I learned about psychology's different branches, its various theories of personality development and functioning. Each branch has its own way of understanding human behavior and conceptualizing personality. These various "schools" of psychological thought are like warring countries, battling over territorial rights to the exclusive possession of the psyche. The arguments are about principles and truth, and they are fought with conviction and fanatical fervor.

A major war exists between the behaviorists and psychoanalysts. While behaviorists focus solely on observables, like behavior and action, psychoanalysts believe in looking at internal events such as feelings, unconscious motivation, and inner conflict. But the fighting isn't limited to these supposedly incompatible ways of thinking about personality development and their implications for psychotherapy. Little wars are waged within these schools. Among the psychoanalysts the arguments are between Freud's libidinally driven view of development and those who see personality as primarily interpersonally determined. Moreover, these battles have their own forms of internal strife, for Kohutians take issue with Sullivanians, and Kleinians quarrel with Freudians.

Although I recognized the differences between these many schools of psychological thought, I felt that there were elements of truth in each. They each have something significant to offer, something that resonated with my understanding of our emotional lives. And while I would have preferred to integrate these aspects, I was expected to take sides and to be indoctrinated into one of the sects.

After completing my coursework, I used a variety of theoretical orientations in my work. I called upon whatever approach seemed applicable at the time. Behavioral techniques were useful in designing treatment programs for children on a hospital ward, and psychoanalytic ideas were helpful in psychotherapy. But when it came time to complete my much belated doctoral dissertation, my adviser insisted that I needed a coat rack, a theoretical framework on which to hang my data.

My dissertation investigated the relationship between physical and emotional space. While I could explain this relationship in everyday terms, I was expected to follow the scientific method by using an existing theory for generating hypotheses and explaining data. I had to make a commitment, even if I felt disinclined to do so, by picking a single existing theory, marrying it, and doing the best I could with it. It was a shotgun wedding. I selected Sullivan's interpersonal theory because it addressed some of the processes I was interested in, but I didn't feel wedded to it.

It has been many years since then. More recently, interest in the psychology of women has spurred a fresh look at development, particularly female development. Previous formulations are now under scrutiny, for most of them were developed by men and, thereby, inadvertently conceptualized from a masculine perspective. We are questioning the underlying assumptions of currently accepted theories, and taking issue with the blatant sexism in concepts such as penis envy, castration anxiety, and the Oedipus complex.

After questioning the more obvious chauvinistic assumptions, we began noticing other issues. Theories are never developed in a vacuum; they are colored by the social climate of the times, its social structure and cultural metaphors. Psychological theory hasn't escaped these influences. Freud's thinking exemplifies such a built-in cultural bias. His concept of the psyche as a battleground for control of instinctual urges reflects its origins in a mechanistic era. It emphasizes the masculine orientation toward control while disregarding the feminine potential for cooperation.

A group of professionals affiliated with the Stone Center of Wellesley College have exposed another masculine bias that is built into many theories of development. Judith Jordan, Alexandra Kaplan, Jean Baker Miller, Irene Stiver, and Janet Surrey (1991) point out that our existing theories of development overvalue movement toward ever-increasing autonomy, toward separation and individuation, while devaluing the more feminine orientation of interpersonal relatedness. Their alternative formulations value the relational aspect of development and focus on the self-in-relation.

While psychologists and other helping professionals are increasingly familiar with Stone Center ideas, our thinking about development is still hampered by preconceived assumptions about development. Living in an unbalanced world, an environment that overvalues the masculine principle at the expense of the feminine, we inadvertently subscribe to a mechanistic view of the universe. Psychology developed within this environment. It grew up with the idea that valid phenomena can be measured in discrete, scientific, standardized units. Because psychological theory uses this yardstick approach when trying to understand human behavior, most theories of development use a linear conception of growth. Life is divided into stages, stepwise progressions along a linear path. These steps are marked by issues or tasks to be addressed and resolved during that stage.

Most psychological formulations assume that human development follows a linear path that moves in one direction or another. Theories differ as to which is the preferred path, the valued goal. One path, favored by the Sullivanians and Stone Center proponents, emphasizes relationships, interpersonal processes, connections with other people, and movement toward others. Another, championed by Mahler and Winnicot, values the process of separating and individuating, the movement toward ever-increasing degrees of autonomy and toward the self. However, an implicit assumption underlies both ways of thinking: Growth entails movement in one direction or another, and one path is more valuable than the other.

I believe that all the important theorists in our field have made significant relevant contributions to our understanding of growth and human development. Each had the benefit of prior conceptualizations, using them as the stepping-off point for their own unique formulations. Often these address the omissions or commissions of previous theories, offering missing pieces to fill in the gaps and complete the puzzle. Our understanding of human behavior has benefitted from each theorist's endeavors.

Our profession struggles to grow, to break free of chains that shackle our minds and blind our thoughts to ideas that may be right in front of our eyes. I believe that as we've been trapped inside western psychology, these shackles have been right under our noses all along. The blinders include our assumption of linearity and the either/or quality of our thought. These characteristics of our mechanistic view of the universe have been all too apparent in our thinking about development.

Moving to Harmony Farm and living cooperatively with nature helped loosen my chains to mechanistic thinking. I became steeped in the natural world, feeling nature's rhythms and cycles. I no longer just read about the balancing interplay of opposites that had attracted me to Oriental philosophy. In addition to observing this interplay, I connected with it. And as I experienced it, felt it inside, something opened inside me. The shackles of mechanistic thinking loosened.

By watching plants grow, I learned the difference between the process and the end product of growth – the difference between growing and grown. I realized that we tend to confuse the two. Our linear conception of growth focuses on the end result, the product. It overlooks the growing process.

Walking through the woods I wondered about growth. I tried to learn nature's secrets and understand her process. Looking up at trees standing straight and tall, it certainly seemed as if they must have grown in a linear fashion. I realized how easy it is to assume that a tree's growth has been unidirectional and linear, that it only grew the way it appears – straight up towards the sun. While the tree is a living picture of some of its growth, it doesn't tell us how it got to be there, the process by which it grew to have its shape.

Even though a plant looks as if it grows straight up, shooting directly toward the sun, time-lapse photography shows that one part, the tip of the stem, is actually growing in spirals. It circles round and around its center, spiralling up towards the sun. If we focus on one end result of growth, it appears linear. However, growth is a process, the process of becoming, of going from here to there. This process is more circular, curvilinear, like a spiral.

By showing me her growing process, nature taught me that human growth has both cyclical and linear qualities. While our development appears linear, for it takes place over time and has direction to its movement, growth itself has a circular quality. It moves ahead in a circular fashion, weaving a spiral web along the way.

Nature's growing process is also a balancing process – an interplay of opposites that includes both masculine (linear) and feminine (circular) elements. Development is multidirectional; it proceeds from a central place of balance, an area of interconnection, a place where opposites come together. This basic dynamic can be observed by paying attention to the way a plant begins to grow.

When a seed germinates it sends a root down to earth, and a stem toward the sun. These two form its center. Any future growth will be connected through this center.

Growth continues in all directions by spreading out from the central stem and central root. While the stem reaches toward the sun, the root provides balance by burrowing into the soil. Other roots develop from the main root and travel down. They tunnel deeper and deeper into the earth, seeking nourishment. Stems branch out above and head into the light. They stretch their leaves toward the sun, absorbing its rays.

The plant continues to grow, requiring sustenance from each direction. Its center expands and grows stronger, fostering growth in every direction and receiving nutrients from each. Nourishment comes from the earth, from the dark soil. The sun offers light. While the branches and leaves depend on the roots to extract vitamins and minerals from the soil, the roots rely on the leaves for photosynthesis. Each direction is necessary, each is essential for growth.

We, too, grow in different directions; we grow out toward other people as well as in toward our selves. Development involves spiralling back and forth between separating and connecting, between individuating and relating. Each movement toward separating and individuating is followed by a new form of connecting. These new forms of relating then enable further development within the self.

Development is a dynamic interplay of many factors that are constantly shifting and changing and moving in different directions. Each psychological theory helps us understand a particular aspect of growth. Portraying a complete picture of development requires integrating what may appear to be divergent approaches. Some formulations have focused on our stems by emphasizing interpersonal processes and the relational aspect. Other conceptualizations have attended to our roots by emphasizing internal processes, inner integration, and autonomy. These various theories complement each other; they each describe necessary aspects of human growth and development.

A whole human being is firmly planted in the soil of the self while branching out, connecting with other people. Our stems and roots keep growing. They spread out from a central place of interconnection, move out from this center in spirals, and wend their way through the cycle of life. They don't move in discrete steps, but in phases that gradually shift and turn. We grow in spirals that are always moving, shifting, and changing.

A spiral is a cycle traveling through time. Its movement extends beyond the circle, never returning to the same place, moving on in time, and moving on in space. This spiral is nature's cycle – the spiral of life, the life cycle.

Stunting

Nothing is perfect in nature. A seed is full of life and will struggle to survive, but there is no such thing as a perfectly formed tree or person. Genetic potentials unfold within environmental contexts.

Development always takes place in a context that fosters and retards growth. Each seed requires an environment that will promote its development by nurturing its particular nature. For example, an acorn, which is capable of developing into a strong tall oak, will remain dormant or fail to thrive in an environment that does not meet its specific needs for earth, water, and sun. Its growth will be stunted by a hostile or otherwise inadequate environment.

Suppressive, inhospitable environments interfere with growth. Branches become gnarled by wind and amputated by heavy snowfall. When other plants and trees block the light, this interferes with growth. Sometimes the earth forms a concrete crust, becoming hard, unyielding, and impenetrable. No roots can burrow in. And while a plant will struggle to overcome such adverse conditions, its growth will be deformed, stunted. It will be unable to fully develop.

Similarly, our environment influences our development. In addition to nature's important elements of earth, sky, and water, we live in a context of other people. Every phase of our development requires someone to nourish, support, or otherwise encourage our growth. And while some adverse conditions offer challenges to growth and novel opportunities for development, overly harsh and repressive environments have the opposite effect. They arrest, impede, and retard development.

As human beings are social animals, our environment is primarily other people. Some of these people, particularly our parents, have a major impact on our development. They influence our identities, they affect who we become. This important aspect of ourselves, our identity, takes shape as our inner potentials unfold within the context of other people.

Even though it is generally assigned to the adolescent "stage," the thread of identity is woven throughout the whole fabric of our lives. Identity issues are present from the beginning to the end of the life cycle, taking on different forms with each developmental phase. Identity is one facet of inner development. It intertwines with other aspects of ourselves, including the capacity to walk.

Who knows when identity begins? While some people believe that past lives influence a present identity, it is probably safe to say that a life begins at conception – when a male sperm joins with a female egg. Nurtured within the mother's body, this life gradually assumes a shape and becomes a recognizable human form with identifiable sex characteristics. This embryo continues growing and developing.

While birth pushes the infant toward separating from Mother, the two remain intertwined. In the world of the infant there is no differentiation between inside and outside. They flow together. Development entails increasing differentiation, both physical and psychological, between inside and outside – learning the difference between what's "me" and what's "not me" (Sullivan, 1953).

Children readily learn what is expected of them. They learn from the adults in their lives. Aspects of themselves that are unacceptable are subsequently separated off, dissociated, from the developing self. These dissociated aspects become part of what has been called the "not-me" – forced underground, relegated to the realm of the dispossessed, the disowned – the unconscious. Through this socialization process children grow into acceptable members of society, at least as interpreted by the significant adults in their environment.

Developing a self takes place in this social context. Children not only learn to behave in an acceptable manner, they continue forming a sense of themselves, of what is "me" and what is "not-me." As "me" is highly influenced by the perceptions of other people, "me" gradually becomes further delineated into "good me" and "bad me" (Sullivan, 1953).

Along the way, "me" learns to walk. This doesn't happen in one day. It begins with a small step that is, in and of itself, a major accomplishment. In developing this ability, the child experiments, trying to discover every detail that goes into making a step. Not knowing how to approach it directly, the child circles round and around, investigating one possibility, then another. The child experiments with foot placement, finding just the right angle and position. As body balance is important, the child gradually learns how to position the head, the arms – all the various body parts. These are just a few of the many inner developments that go into executing the first big step.

Once the child takes one step, then another and another, walking becomes possible. Learning to walk, which is an internal process, shifts the child's relationship with other people. These steps open the door to a wider world of opportunity. The child can move independently toward another person, one step after another, and reach out to hand that person a little red rubber ball. The child can give. Or, depending upon environmental circumstances, the child might prefer to move away from someone, taking one step after another. Choice becomes possible.

These, and a myriad of other developmental processes, continue through early childhood as identity moves into the next phase, forming an "I." The childhood phase focuses on nurturing the "I," enabling it to become increasingly delineated. Each aspect of inner development is matched by shifts outside the self, with other people. The child forms a relationship with one peer, then with others. One "step" leads to another and another. Each inner shift is followed by an outward step, gradually widening the circle of relationships, both internal and external.

Adolescence loops around, repeating an earlier theme. During this phase "I" develops definition and gradually moves toward separation from parental figures. Putting first one foot in front and then the other, the "child" eventually moves out of the house to live independently of parental figures.

Identity development continues throughout adulthood. The "I" often branches out into work, spouse, children, and grandchildren. And, as our lives come full circle, to the final phase, we often gradually lose our identities and become increasingly less differentiated. Death brings loss of self, non-identity . . . re-entering a state of non-being . . . completing the life cycle.

The thread of identity weaves its way through the life cycle, intertwining with other strands to create the fabric of a life. Along the way some strands are nourished, encouraged to develop. Other

Healing

When I was a young girl I read *Heidi*, by Johanna Spyri. The book's images resonated inside me. Imagining myself to be Heidi, I ran barefoot through meadows, felt damp grass under my feet, smelled sweet mountain air, and gleefully picked bunches of wild-flowers. I fell in love with mountains.

The story was still fresh in my memory when my parents took us to the Swiss Alps for a family holiday. There, with great trepidation, I learned to ski. I enjoyed breathing fresh mountain air, feeling it expand in my lungs. The sunlight was brighter than bright. It reflected off the snow, bouncing in every direction. The world was shining, shimmering, glistening. I felt an inner glow and, again, fell in love with mountains. They rose majestically out of the ground, towering over our heads. Their white peaks unforgettably contrasted against deep blue sky. I was captivated by mountains.

Since then, there have been many occasions when my mind drifted back to those towers of white outlined by blue, with puffs of white cotton wool floating in the distance. I heard the mountains calling, and wanted to run to them. This usually happened during my troubled times – times when whirling sensations ran riot throughout my body and mind, when confusion and chaos reigned within.

For years I thought it was the mountains that beckoned and called. Then I fell in love with the ocean. While walking on the beach, listening to waves rippling in and out, breathing moist salty air, and hearing sounds of sea gulls, I felt whole and complete. My heart expanded, filling every corner of my body. I felt centered and serene.

Then I had a similar experience in a meadow. I danced among tall grasses, captured wildflowers in my hands, and wound them into a garland to wear on my head. I felt ecstatic, at one with myself, at peace with the world – whole.

Gradually, it dawned on me that these places were healing places. They were healing because of the overwhelming presence of nature. These were places where I felt her presence. She became part of my inner being, correcting whatever imbalance was there – creating wholeness where there was division, balance where I was off center.

I have come to understand that *Heidi* and similar tales, such as *The Secret Garden* by Frances Hodgson Burnett, are about the healing powers of nature. If it weren't for nature, physical and emotional wounds would be unable to heal. Nature provides the resources that make it possible for us to recover from injuries.

Nature's resources include both the masculine and the feminine. Nature is, therefore, active as well as passive, linear as well as circular, nurturing as well as punitive, hot as well as cold, and light as well as dark. Nature is heaven and earth, sun and moon, night and day, life and death.

Nature's way is that of heterogeneity, balance, and harmony. Unlike the assembly line, carbon-copied products of mechanization, she presents herself in all kinds of shapes, sizes, colors, and textures. Males and females are both represented in nature. Androgyny, heterosexuality, homosexuality, and bisexuality are all found in nature. And while diversity is one of the most noticeable characteristics of nature, natural environments are also balanced. Masculine and feminine processes constantly balance each other, creating a whole.

Wherever I walk, whether in a forest or along a beach, I cannot help but observe that each area has its own wildflowers, each of which grows in an environment that fosters its growth. No two plants and no two areas are exactly the same. And no two moments are ever the same, for nature is in perpetual motion, always shifting, always changing.

Whenever I take the same path over a period of time, I watch the changes taking place. Sometimes the movement is gradual, almost imperceptible. At other times, like in the wake of a thunderstorm or hurricane, change is sudden, more dramatic. Regardless of the type of change, the same process is taking place. It is a process whereby any change in ecological balance is offset by a counterbalancing adjustment, which then sets the stage for the next shift. It is an open system, ever ready to react to a new influence, to an unexpected turn of events.

Nature moves towards balance. Balance isn't a fixed static state. It is full of movement and activity – a perpetual dance – a balancing act between parts that are constantly moving to correct an imbalance.

Part of the movement toward balance is that movement we call healing. Healing is one aspect of a system moving to correct an imbalance in another, so that the system itself is perpetuated, the imbalance remedied.

As we are part of nature, we participate in her processes. We feel psychologically well when we are emotionally balanced – when we are in tune with ourselves and centered, as well as connected with other people. Similarly, we feel physically well when our bodies are in a balanced state, when there is no major physiological disharmony. Dis-ease involves a disruption of balance. Until the imbalance is remedied we say that we are sick.

Our bodies are one aspect of this natural system. They are built with many internal checks and balances; an imbalance in one area is responded to and remedied. Our bodies aim to maintain health, equilibrium, and balance. We feel unwell when their various balancing tactics, their defense mechanisms, are overwhelmed and become unable to exert their healing influence.

People usually can't describe how they get better. Healing occurs outside consciousness, outside awareness, outside rational, reasoning thought. It occurs at deeper levels, levels of ourselves that connect with nature – the physical and emotional aspects of ourselves that are our inner nature.

Healing is always in the hands of nature. Surgeons are adept at removing diseased organs, repairing damaged tissue, and replacing defective parts. They help correct structural problems. But once the surgeon finishes suturing, it is up to the body to heal – to recover from surgery and restore functioning.

People intuitively seek out the mountains or the seaside for rest cures. Long before the development of modern medicine people travelled to these places in order to feel better. And people did get better, returning home "cured." Nowadays we call these rest cures vacations, knowing that they give us an opportunity to rejuvenate our bodies, our minds, and our spirits.

Today's scientists might attribute these "cures" to the placebo effect. I believe that we need to understand the placebo effect, ask how and why it works, not merely dispose of *it* in the wastepaper basket. I suspect these cures are natural happenings, times when nature has been given an opportunity to correct an imbalance, to heal it. Resting allows time for our inner resources – masculine and feminine processes that are our innate healing abilities – to fulfill their potential. Nature then has an opportunity to exert her healing influence.

Nature's rhythms, cycles, and balancing processes are our healing resources. After spending millions of dollars on scientific research, we have learned more and more about this healing process. We've labelled it our immune system, a fancy label for nature's way of keeping us healthy, nature's way of correcting imbalances. In this case, at least we recognize that it is a system, that there is a process involved. All too often the medical community thinks in terms of symptoms, end results of the process by which the system became imbalanced. "Cures" are directed toward symptoms, observable difficulties, rather than the underlying processes creating the difficulty.

Whenever we define an ailment as a sore throat, a heart problem, an eating disorder, depression, or an ulcer, we are describing a symptom – not the real difficulty necessarily, but the observable end result of whatever imbalance is contributing to the symptom.

Our social orientation is toward quick fixes and immediate solutions. Visits to doctors are expected to result in prescriptions for medications that will alleviate the problem. Medicine can often be of help. In the situation where a sore throat is diagnosed as due to a streptococcus infection, penicillin can render the pathogen harmless. But it is then up to the body to do the healing, to recover from the imbalance, to return to health.

Medication serves as a palliative solution. While it may effectively deal with a symptom, it generally does not resolve the underlying problem that enabled the symptom to develop. Contrary to what we're led to believe, a headache is not a sign of an aspirin deficiency. Furthermore, taking aspirin to eradicate a headache may further mask the underlying problem, one that might lead to more serious difficulties unless it is addressed and attended to. Similarly, taking penicillin doesn't deal with the underlying imbalance that enabled an infection to develop. All too often, people mistakenly believe that "the problem" has been resolved by surgery or medication. We are lulled into thinking we've regained health when we've merely managed to eliminate symptoms.

Another way of looking at symptoms is to work with the underlying processes contributing to the difficulty. Disease-promoting processes need to be reversed, health and well-being need to be promoted, and balance needs to be reinstated. And one obvious, but frequently overlooked, issue concerns whether the body-mind system has been given the kind of assistance that facilitates nature's healing processes.

Nature does not operate according to fast-paced time schedules. It takes time, sometimes a long time, for an imbalanced system to develop a symptom; similarly it takes time for balance to be reinstated. This can take years, not days, and may involve lifestyle changes that some people are not inclined to make.

Part of the difficulty, as I see it, is that we have moved from a naturalistic way of viewing the world to a mechanistic one. We think in mechanical terms and look at ourselves as if we were machines, as if we were built of interchangeable, replaceable parts. We no longer think of ourselves as one of nature's beings.

We have drifted further and further away from nature's rhythms, and are increasingly out of sync with our natural healing resources. Our environment is polluted. Our bodies are struggling to cope with unnatural substances they cannot help but inhale or ingest. No wonder there has been such a dramatic increase in the number of allergy complaints over the years, for allergies are immune system symptoms. It also comes as no surprise to me that the dreaded fatal diseases of our society, cancer and AIDS, are immune system problems. These are just a few of the "diseases" that are symptomatic of immune system dysfunction.

Our immune systems are letting us know that something is wrong, that our natural healing resources are unable to keep up with the demands being placed on them. We have drifted too far from nature's healing ways. Our medicine has lost its connection with natural processes. We've been swallowing medicine rather than listening to symptoms.

A healing therapy delves deeper. It uses nature's healing resources, works with underlying processes, and addresses the roots of the difficulty, the factors contributing to the problem. It concerns itself with the whole health of a person – the physical, the spiritual, and the psychological. And it aims to balance masculine with feminine.

Tools

Space

Therapists promote growth by working with the environment. Recognizing the parallels between physical and psychological space, we look to create conditions conducive to growth. We attend to the spatial dimensions of our clients' inner and outer worlds.

Most therapists recognize that the design of an office can influence therapy. As confidentiality is essential, we guard the privacy of our offices with soundproofing devices such as double doors and sound shields. We also pay attention to the seating arrangement, among other details, making sure that it communicates an atmosphere of intimacy while affording clients a sense of safety and respect for their boundaries and personal comfort.

I believe that the importance of working in harmony with nature can also be communicated to clients. Although I am not suggesting that every therapist's office should be in a natural setting, I personally prefer working in close proximity to nature. Harmony Farm's setting not only keeps me in tune with nature's healing processes, it also sets the tone for my clients. And it subtly invites them to pay attention to their sensory experiences.

A rural mailbox marks the entrance to Harmony Farm. Clients turn off a heavily traveled suburban road onto a dirt driveway. They're entering another world, moving into a sacred place.

Once off the road, clients are transported into an idyllic rural setting. As they wend their way along the winding drive, they're surrounded by nature. Stands of trees are punctuated by open spaces with wild vegetation.

Clients usually slow their cars to negotiate the unpaved path. This gives them time to notice the seasons, to watch them pass by, for the cycle from leaf to flower to fruit to seed is ever apparent along this drive. During fall the trees boast shimmering shades of red, orange, and yellow. Once their leaves descend to earth, they become graceful brown silhouettes, perfect contrasts against the glistening snow of a winter's day. Green returns when skunk cabbage makes its appearance in early spring, a welcome sign that daisies and daylilies will soon be on their way.

Sheep graze in the meadow – a perpetual source of entertainment. Their thick woolly coverings offer protection from the ravages of weather, even harsh cold wintry winds. Although the sheep are wary of cars, they are curious to see who may be passing by and often lift their heads from the task of satisfying healthy appetites. During spring and summer they often resemble a giant lawn mower, lined up one next to the other, moving ahead slowly, step by step, leaving shorn grass in their wake.

After lambing season, in early spring, sheep-watching becomes irresistible. Cars automatically slow to a snail's pace so their occupants can get a better view. Lambs capture everyone's heart. They're full of boundless energy, leaping and bouncing, expressing their spirited lust for life and joy of discovery.

When it is time to nurse, patient mothers stand calmly chewing their cud while exuberant lambs forcefully butt their heads into the mothers' abdomens. This activity signals the mothers to release milk into their udders. The lambs fall to their knees, attach themselves to udders, and eagerly guzzle life-giving juices.

Tearing themselves away from the sheep, clients continue their journey by heading toward a barn. As chickens range freely in this area, they may need to stop their cars to allow one to safely scurry out of the way. After passing the barn, a house soon comes into view. My herb garden, replete with additional wildflowers and an assortment of weeds, is on their left as they turn toward the house and park the car. Once out of the car they may pause to savor the smell of pine wafting through the air. Depending on the season, other aromas may also greet them.

A flagstone path leads the way to the office entrance. Thyme grows between the stones, spreading its tendrils in all directions. Even the most careful clients can't avoid stepping on the thyme, releasing its aromatic oils and distinctive aroma. As they walk to the door, they're surrounded by muted hues and subtle smells, with birds singing in the background.

The outside door opens to a set of stairs that lead to a small waiting area. There is classical music playing in the background, hot water ready for a cup of herbal tea, and magazines proclaiming the joys of country living waiting to be read. A "thank you for not smoking" sign shines forth from the bulletin board, and a herbal chart of natural remedies adorns the wall.

Inside the office, plants are everywhere. Each flowering season is gaily represented, creating a year-round profusion of blooming color. Christmas and orchid cactuses hang from pottery baskets attached to the ceiling. Medicinal aloe plants multiply in pots on top of a table. Cyclamen galore, along with various Thanksgiving, Christmas, and Easter cactuses sit on bookcases beneath two large southern windows that overlook a pond. There are vibrant pinks, purples, and reds through fall, winter, spring, and summer – a perfect foil for blue skies and white bookcases. The room is bright with light, alive with color, yet calm and still.

My office is a safe place, an inner sanctum. I sit here with clients, enter their space, and help them wrestle with their issues. This is a physical space – a place where they come with their difficulties, a place where they can begin paying attention to themselves. My office is protected space – a place reserved for them – offering peace and quiet for listening to concerns, voicing them, and having them heard.

I see it as my responsibility to ensure that clients' sessions are their sacred space. I protect this space and insure no intrusions, no ringing telephones, no interruptions. They are away from the demands of their lives, their jobs, families, friends, society. It is their time – time to devote to themselves in whichever way is most useful to them. It is precious time, and I protect it.

Clients usually need to begin experiencing their value, their worth – to respect themselves and their time. As I want them to know that I honor their therapy time, I endeavor to be punctual for appointments. Keeping clients waiting would be not only impolite, inconsiderate, and disrespectful, it also implies that their time doesn't matter whereas mine does. I won't do them a disservice by keeping them waiting.

Once they're inside the office, clients have a chance to pause, take a breath, and travel inside themselves. Many arrive breathless from a morning of getting children ready for school or dealing with issues at work. Often when they arrive, head dizzy with all the doings they've just left behind, they need to slow down and become still. Then, and only then, can they begin focusing in, listening to an inner voice.

I've learned to be quiet – to allow space between a client's sentences and between us. This space is especially important at the beginning of a session. It enables clients to settle in – to wind down, then in – to enter the space inside themselves.

Sometimes clients arrive saying, "I have nothing to talk about today" or "on my way over I was wondering about what I would talk about." Once they're given the time to sit quietly with themselves, subjects invariably present themselves. Issues that were beneath the surface begin bubbling up.

At times, clients anticipate their sessions and use the drive over as a time to slow down and begin focusing inward. This usually isn't done with conscious forethought. They begin their sessions by commenting about the drive, their thoughts along the way. We go on together from there. And when they leave, they take the stillness with them. Images, symbols, and thoughts addressed during a session continue to reverberate during the drive home, later in the day, and throughout the week.

Clients need to enter their quiet, peaceful, inner place before they can begin hearing themselves. All too often their fast-paced lives don't allow time for stillness. They're focused outside themselves, bombarded by demands – communications from people, the media, the telephone ringing. Moving into stillness is a necessary precursor for other shifts, for creative internal moments, change. It initiates the shifting process.

Therapy is defined by its protected time and place. It provides a safe, predictable place where time can stand still – an environment for change. The safety of this time and place enables the space, the stillness, the precursor of other shifts. This protected space needs to be reserved on a regular basis, for predictability contributes to its safety.

All the details of time and place set the stage, prime the pump, facilitate the process of moving into stillness. And as this happens, other shifts become possible. Time slows down, becoming ever more still until a doorway in time opens. Past, present, and future combine in a fleeting eternal moment, a moment of connection. This is sacred space.

Sacred space is timeless. It exists in the "betweens" – between here and there, known and unknown, conscious and unconscious, creation and destruction, good and evil, life and death. Shifts take place in spaces, in betweens, in twilight zones. Sacred space is a place of shifting sands, a place where disparate forces combine in new and novel ways – sublime moments of association.

Momentary though they may be, these between times can be unsettling. The ground is no longer steady and firm, but moving and transforming. Clients sometimes describe themselves as feeling adrift on a sea, floating. They look for an anchor, a place of mooring. At these times I offer myself as their anchor – a place of settledness, stillness, silence. And while I offer my center, my space, as a place of mooring from which we can both operate during the hour, I gently invite them to become anchored within themselves, to sense firm ground under their feet.

Sacred space is inside and outside. It's a womb – a place for creation, union, giving birth. Clients give birth to themselves, and we're midwives in this process, the timekeepers. Our job is to help them move into sacred space – help slow down time.

Therapy occurs in a space between two people, but the main work is done inside one person. Our role as therapists is to provide an environment that fosters growth – *their* growth. In fulfilling this function we attend to all the dimensions of time and space. We nurture their space, tend its garden, ensure that there's adequate moisture, sunlight, and nourishment.

The seeds are within our clients. They're waiting for the right conditions, for a fertile environment in which to send out roots and unfurl leaves. It takes time for seeds to germinate and for growth to unfold. We wait and watch, offering comments here and there, nourishing growth. And while we may help by nurturing the soil, cultivating an area, we cannot make seeds grow. We're only caretakers of the environment, guardians of sacred space.

The therapeutic journey is a long and winding path, punctuated by brief excursions into sacred space. Clients are free to focus on their journey, be fully present in it, knowing that someone else is ensuring its safety. We're overseers – waiting and watching while clients maneuver through their journeys' twists and turns.

Clients need time for their symbols to incubate, to mull around in the unconscious, and allow new ways to gradually emerge. There may be a momentary "ah ha," but these are few and far between. Instead, there are little "ahs," pauses for internal mulling, shifting, moving. These serpentine shifts slowly weave together and evolve into a spiral path.

And as clients take this path, their perspectives change. They emerge from cotyledons, like butterflies from cocoons, ready to flower and fly. And when they reflect upon their journey, they comment on the sense of peace and tranquility that descends upon them the moment they turn into the driveway. They've been enveloped in nature's silent stillness, the magic of Harmony Farm.

Relationship

Most therapists believe that the relationship we develop with clients is an important therapeutic tool. And while we generally also concur regarding the inappropriateness of sexual intimacy with clients, there is less agreement about the type of therapist involvement most beneficial to client growth and healing. This issue affects many aspects of therapy, including the names we call ourselves and whether we purposefully reveal personal information.

More traditional, psychoanalytically based, models recommend maintaining an impersonal stance with clients, one which facilitates the development and analysis of transference. Earlier relationships, particularly those between parent and child, are re-created in the interest of separating past from present and offering a corrective educational experience. Many therapists, myself included, were schooled in this tradition. Within this model we also expected clients to use our formal titles, e.g., Dr. Shore, rather than our first names, and avoided sharing personal information about ourselves.

My early years as a therapist were spent hiding behind a blank screen. While most of my training was in psychoanalytic psychotherapy, I was also influenced by existential analysis and nondirective counseling. As I was committed to becoming a good therapist, I endeavored to practice what my teachers, supervisors, and books preached. I went by the book, and the books of those times proselytized the fine art of noninvolvement.

While I listened intently to clients, integrating and paraphrasing what I heard, I did not allow any aspect of myself to be revealed. I became adept at ducking questions, deflecting them back to clients. It was like playing hide-and-seek. Whenever they tried to find out who I was, I hid. I either dodged behind an interpretation or "answered" their question with another question. And when clients developed relationships with me, I saw our relationships in terms of transference and countertransference phenomena.

After working in college counseling centers, I was hired as the psychologist on the treatment team of a new detoxification ward for drug addicts and alcoholics. Working with these people required a different approach. I had to literally think on my feet, for many of these clients approached me in the hallway when I was en route from one place to another. While I also had an office, I could no longer hide behind its closed door or the blank screen that was available there. I immediately recognized that my clients were better at dancing around bushes than I, for they had been on their toes much longer, and playing for much higher stakes. These people required a more direct approach, one that encouraged them to face issues they preferred to avoid. Although I continued to dodge and duck, I developed a different style for working with this population. I became more direct, up front, and outspoken.

Continuing with my professional career, I moved from one clinical setting to another, adapting my style of therapy to the people with whom I was working. As I gained confidence in my clinical judgement and therapeutic skills, I started trusting my own sense of the therapy situation. Questions and comments often came from my "gut," not just my head. And while it had felt safer to hide during my early years as a therapist, I no longer needed to hide. My relationship with clients grew more open and natural. I cared deeply about them and knew that they felt my warmth.

Even though my heart was telling me that warm, caring relationships are healing, intellectually I still adhered to the principles of the psychoanalytic approach and believed in the usefulness of the blank screen. I felt conflicted, and questioned the value of staying uninvolved, disconnected from clients. My heart and head were split.

My questions continued, particularly after becoming a wife and then mother. These caretaking roles pulled me in another direction, toward the physical realm. Feeling responsible for the welfare of people I loved and wanting to ensure their health and well-being, I began reading about nutrition and visiting health food stores. My interest in health didn't follow the traditional path, for I consumed books on medicinal herbs and old-fashioned "home" remedies. And when kissing a child seemed able to make everything "better,"

I became intrigued with the body-mind connection and wondered if there could be a curative aspect to caring.

While I was pleased to see my family benefitting from these explorations into holistic health, I felt split between two worlds. In my home I was a nurturing, giving, and loving human being. But these emotions were considered "inappropriate" in the traditional therapeutic session where I wanted to be able to share my knowledge about health and well-being without compromising my uninvolved, disengaged, professional stance.

Hearing about a new field, behavioral medicine, which legitimized my interest in the mind-body connection, I began taking seminars and attending conferences on the subject. One was organized by Beth Israel Hospital, a respected teaching hospital affiliated with Harvard Medical School. Dr. Herbert Benson, a cardiologist already well known for his books, especially *The Relaxation Response*, was a featured speaker.

After registering, I was approached by a smiling man who welcomed me to the conference and introduced himself as "Herb Benson." We talked for a while, and during this conversation he happened to touch my shoulder. His touch wasn't sexual, but a connection, a bridge between us. Walking away from this meeting I felt special, cared about, "touched."

This meeting with Herb Benson made a lasting impression. I remember him as a man radiating warmth, gentleness, compassion, and caring. His physical touch had reached inside me, warmed me. It showed he cared about connecting and told me more about the mind-body connection than was later communicated in many hours of well organized, dynamic presentations.

When I returned to my office, I began thinking about the role of touch in therapy. While touch has a long history in the healing professions, it is a complicated topic. Touch can be confused with sexuality, especially by people who have difficulty distinguishing between different kinds of feelings. Because of the highly intimate nature of psychological material, the potential abuse of touch, and the importance of psychological boundaries for vulnerable clients, the role of touch requires careful consideration.

Continuing to mull about these issues, I realized that Herb Benson's touch was connected to his caring. I had responded to Herb's openness and his caring, not just his touch. His caring felt healing.

In trying to sort out my feelings about the therapeutic relationship, I turned to books such as *Woman as Healer* by Jeanne Achterberg, *Healing Wise* by Susan Weed, and *For Her Own Good* by Barbara Ehrenreich and Deirdre English. These books, along with others by French (1985), Gimbutas (1982, 1989) and Stone (1976), helped place my thoughts within a historical perspective. I realized that my concerns were one facet of a larger issue that involves different ways of conceptualizing the role of the healer.

Most ways of thinking about the healing process recognize that healing often occurs in relationship. The doctor-patient relationship is a more recent form of healing relationship. Ever since the mind-body split, spiritual healing has been mainly managed by men. Physical healing initially remained in the hands of women. These women healers could trace their heritage to ancient healing practices of the wise woman tradition.

The wise woman tradition is an old tradition. Its roots travel back to at least 25,000 BC, a time when we paid homage to an immanent Mother Earth goddess and saw ourselves as intertwined with nature (Gimbutas, 1982, 1989). Healing was linked with the tasks and spirit of motherhood. This nurturing model relied on sensory observation and intuition for gathering information which was handed down from one generation to the next. And although wise women frequently administered herbal remedies, whole natural substances, they also typically remained with their patients during the healing process, touching them, and connecting with them in a variety of ways.

Although the feminine model of healing has been subjugated by the masculine, relegated to a lowly status, it hasn't been totally lost. Midwives, nurses, and other practitioners combine wisdom with nurturance, and tenderness with skill (Ehrenreich & English, 1979). They remain close to their clients – connected, involved.

Many people still think that medicine's best practitioners were the old-fashioned family doctors – people who got involved, cared. Although those physicians were scientifically schooled, they were also rooted in the feminine tradition. But as the masculine model became more and more entrenched, these physicians became rare breeds, replaced by specialists who dissect our bodies into increasingly smaller, more manageable, parts. As these specialists worship the scientific method, they aspire to be impartial and objective. Trying to cultivate a sterile, clean atmosphere, they disconnect from their patients. And because psychoanalysis also developed within the medical model, its children and grandchildren inherited a tradition that values distance and objectivity, the blank screen.

The masculine model of healing bequeaths a difficult role to every practitioner. We've inherited a tradition that splits heaven from earth and mind from body. We're expected to direct our attention toward one small segment of the whole, systematically analyze the difficulty, and treat the problem. And, most importantly, we're expected to keep feelings from influencing our judgement. We are to be scientific.

Despite our best intentions, practicing therapists can't be completely disconnected, uninvolved, or impartial. As we are human beings, not machines, we become involved with clients. But because of the masculine model, we aim to be totally objective and struggle against our natural inclination to care. Some therapists become detached, even aloof, through their efforts to live up to this ideal.

However, psychotherapy is changing. Irene Stiver (1991) has written about reframing treatment models, rethinking the meaning of "care." Judith Jordan (1991) and Jean Baker Miller (1976, 1986, 1987b) stress the important role of mutuality in any healthy relationship, including the therapeutic one. Empathy has been given a valid place in the therapeutic setting (Jordan, Surrey, & Kaplan, 1991). These and other feminist therapists have been challenging the masculine model, questioning its assumptions, and suggesting an infusion of feminine values, particularly the one of caring-connection.

During times of change we're prone to swing from one extreme to the other. By challenging the masculine model, feminist therapists offer a valuable perspective. But if we reject the masculine model, we will pay another price, for it also has something to offer. Unfortunately, many therapists are caught in the trap I found myself struggling with – torn between masculine and feminine models, split between heart and mind, body and soul.

We get into deep water whenever we create artificial dichotomies. As opposites complement each other, balance each other, and create a whole, therapists needn't be separate or connected, involved or uninvolved. We can be both!

I'm of most help to clients when I'm fully myself. Although I believe that it's not useful for clients to know the intimate details of my life, I do want them to feel connected with a whole person, a real human being. And while it's important that I maintain a professional stance, I can also be involved with clients, smile at them, laugh with them, nurture them, and genuinely care about them.

Impartial attitudes perpetuate the status quo, especially in a society where the feminine is not only devalued but equated with gender. Females are disempowered, also abused. We dissociate from our selves. Males suppress feelings. In order to redress these conditions, therapists must abandon the position of disinterested bystanders and become advocates for the feminine. This often means helping women feel entitled, and encouraging men to own their feelings. By engaging with clients, we become advocates for their lost voices, the neglected aspects of society, and also their selves.

As a healing relationship must be responsive to the needs of each client in each moment and in each session, we're of most use to clients when we allow each situation to determine the nature of our interaction. I try to offer myself in whatever way is most therapeutically useful, tailoring therapy to the needs of each client, addressing each person's unique dimensions in a manner that is best suited to him or her.

While it's helpful for clients to feel connected with us, supported by us, nourished by the relationship, it's generally useful if we step out of their pictures and help them find their own answers. Our leading questions point to a direction, usually back toward their selves.

Sometimes we may decide to share information, to not sidestep a question but answer it. We serve as guides for their journeys by sharing our thoughts on issues and offering our personal perspectives, another view to consider. But ultimately it is our clients' journeys. They see the road in front of them, and only they can decide which fork to take. All we can do is make sure we're with them every step of the way.

The therapeutic relationship is the soil of therapy, an environment for growth. That soil can't be sterile or empty, for proper nourishment is a prerequisite for growth, and starvation only stunts. While at times the soil requires watering, at other times it needs fertilizing. There are also times to wait and watch, allowing seeds to germinate, ideas to incubate, and fruit to set. Each gardening deed is helpful in its own time and in due order; none is helpful if overdone and relied upon to the excess of all others.

If we keep our minds and hearts open, we will be able to give the soil what it needs. But if we limit what we put into the soil, we limit the nutrients available for growth. A soil rich in many elements helps clients develop their dormant seeds and the stunted parts of their selves.

Language

When I became a psychologist I never expected that my work would involve travelling to different worlds, and I didn't realize that I would be required to speak a variety of languages. If I had known this ahead of time, I would probably have sought another profession, for language had never been my forte. In contrast to my parents who had grown up in Europe, were seasoned travellers, and fluent in five languages, my exposure to foreign languages took place inside books and classrooms. After limping my way through this educational process, I developed a sense of myself as deficient in whatever it took to learn languages. I saw myself as having a language disability.

When I started practicing psychotherapy it rapidly became apparent that language would be an essential aspect of my work, a therapeutic tool. Even if my clients spoke English, I would need to learn their particular language in order to communicate with them. And even if my foreign language skills were purported to be poor, I would be travelling in different worlds and would need to learn the languages of these areas.

I now realize that part of my language disability was due to the fact that it is difficult to learn language from sterile lists of conjugated verbs and translated meanings. Language is part of the communication process. It is the medium for communication inside ourselves as well as with other people, for it shapes our ideas and thoughts while providing the form for their expression. Without language we'd be unable to talk with one another. And the best way to learn a language is by using it to communicate with other people.

Language is the form in which information is encoded, stored, and decoded. Most living beings have a type of language. Their senses take in information from the environment and encode it using a form of language. This encoded information is then transmitted and acted upon in some way, possibly stored.

Even non-living things can have language. Computers are our most important tools for dealing with information. They encode information, store it, and decode it in a language I have yet to understand. Luckily I have a computer that is comparatively user-friendly.

We learn our native language during our early years. After mastering the basics of that language, we learn the subtleties, the nuances, the underlying meanings. The ethos of our culture, its mythology, is woven within our language. This language plays an important role in shaping cognition and perception. It molds the way we experience our world – the way we think, feel, and act.

Living in America, it's easy to forget the importance of language. We all generally speak the same language, even if our accents belie present and past residences. We take language for granted and travel to other countries without being able to speak their languages.

I was one such ugly American when I travelled to France with my brother and his wife for a skiing vacation. My foreign language skills were practically nonexistent when it came to French; I only knew a few basic words, the equivalents of *yes*, *no*, and *thank you*. My brother was quite adept at turning a French phrase, so I knew I could count on his translations. I, therefore, blithely packed a suitable array of French-English phrase books and headed for the Alps.

All went well as long as I was with my brother and his wife. About halfway through our vacation, our legs tired from their daily burdens of negotiating the slopes. As the weather also took a turn for the worse, we decided to take a day off the slopes and give our legs a rest. This was the perfect opportunity for me to roam around town, get a feel for the area, cash traveller's checks, and buy some French souvenirs, clothes. I bravely bid *adieu* to my brother and, with phrase books in hand, headed off on my own.

Almost immediately, I became lost. I wasn't physically lost, but I felt lost. As I didn't speak French, I didn't have the fundamental tools for gathering information. The usually simple act of asking a question was practically an impossibility. I didn't know where I was and I couldn't ask.

Since I couldn't communicate with words, I needed to find another language, another form of communication. Recognizing that nonverbal ways of relating are more universal than verbal ones,

I tried using my body to express what I was trying to say and began gesticulating with my hands. Thanks to expressive hands, my visit to the bank was successful and I was able to cash some traveller's checks. However, negotiating the stores was more difficult, for the information I wished to convey was far more complicated.

I began using my whole body to communicate. My fingers pointed, my shoulders shrugged, my head nodded and shook. After a while my whole body was called into play as I pantomimed my requests.

Although my body could communicate quite a bit of what I wanted to say, my troubles weren't over. Once the salespeople gathered what I was trying to tell them, their comprehension was relayed by an excited "Ah," followed by a rapid rush of French words, gestures, and smiles. Even if I had been able to understand a few words, I couldn't keep up with their pace. The words flew past me. Before I could catch up with one phrase, another went rushing by. I was thoroughly confused. Finally they took pity on me and resorted to using the language we had in common. Gestures replaced tongues, and my shopping spree wasn't quite the catastrophe it could have become.

My trip to France taught me an important lesson. If I want to communicate with someone, I need to be fluent in their language. I couldn't speak French, but there was another, more fundamental, language we shared. Body language is universal. It is embedded deep within the human psyche, and is one of the languages of psychotherapy. And while I didn't have my parents' background of travelling to different countries, working in a variety of clinical settings has helped me learn the languages of psychotherapy.

Psychotherapy is a journey into the domain of the psyche. In order to take this journey, to communicate with the inhabitants of the psyche, we need to speak its language. And while there are no good topographical maps of the area, Freud described three general regions: the conscious, the preconscious, and the unconscious. In addition, he suggested that these areas have two different languages. While secondary process is the language of more conscious, rational thought, the unconscious uses primary process language.

Secondary process is the language I am using now. Its definitions are clearly defined and consensually validated. It's more conscious, more rational, and follows laws of syntax and logic. As this is the language we use every day, we tend to be more familiar with it, more comfortable in it. It's the backbone of communication.

While secondary process is primarily a verbal language, primary process is more often nonverbal. It is symbolic language, the language of dreams, fantasy, and other reverie. Symbolic language is the language of the body. It speaks in pictures, smells, sounds, feelings, tastes – all forms of physical sensation. This language is more loosely connected, more associative, less logical. It's a metaphorical, timeless language, for unconscious processes don't differentiate between past, present, and future. In addition, multiple meanings are woven together, merged within one symbol. There is no one true meaning, only meaningful connections of meaning.

Erich Fromm wrote about this language of inner experience. He called it the forgotten language because most of us tend to forget this language when we are awake. Yet he felt that symbolic language is "the one foreign language that each of us must learn" (Fromm, 1951, p. 10). It is the one language that all people, across all cultures, have in common. Being able to communicate in this language puts us in touch with deeper regions of the human psyche.

While I had read about symbolic, primary process language in psychology class, used it to interpret poems in English class, and tried to apply it in understanding my own dreams, I would never have become facile at hearing this language without one particular experience. Early in my career I fortuitously accepted a position working with severely disturbed, hospitalized children and adolescents. Many were psychotic, which means that their thinking is disturbed. Their thoughts aren't logically connected, but flow into each other in an associative way. As I needed to be able to communicate with them, I had to learn their language.

Psychotic language is symbolic, concrete, and synergistically determined. It is similar to the language of poems and dreams, closely approximating primary process thought. I felt as if I were living in another country and had been given an opportunity to learn its language. It was a challenge to understand and be understood.

While at first I felt lost, adrift in an alien land, my more experienced colleagues showed me how to hear this language. Though in formal meetings, we played with words, punned. I was reminded of happy times from my youth, sitting around the dinner table, similarly playing with words. Inviting my mind to associate and pun, I rediscovered the pleasure of playing with the twists and turns of language.

My style of therapy changed. While my roots burrowed deeper into the analytic tradition, I also branched out, exploring some more feminine ways of communicating with these children and adolescents. As art is one form of symbolic expression, I kept my office well stocked with blank paper, crayons, and pencils, and I often invited them to paint or draw. Their pictures were worth more than the proverbial thousand words. And, like myself in France, they also communicated with their bodies. Some of them, the autistic children, seemed to live in another world and to communicate only with their bodies.

We had one 13-year-old youngster, Peter,* who was autistic. His behavior was often aggressive and physically destructive. While he seemed to understand what others said to him, he rarely spoke, let alone used words in a logical sequence. He often came into the ward meeting, which all the children and adolescents were invited to attend. At times he left shortly thereafter, but sometimes he just sat and rocked. As long as his rocking didn't interfere with the meeting, I welcomed his presence in the room.

On one particular occasion, Peter came into the ward meeting and sat down without rocking. After a while he began to clap, a rhythmic clap, for autistic children are apt to follow a rhythm. Instead of asking him to leave, I decided to wait and see what would happen next. It didn't take long. Soon everyone in the room started to clap. The clapping followed his rhythm, which he changed from time to time. Each time he changed the rhythm of his clap all the clapping followed suit. This communication process continued for a while, and then stopped.

Peter's rhythmic clapping was his way of communicating with us. The others heard his message and responded. They were willing to "speak" his language, even if they didn't understand what it meant. He became part of the group.

---

*I've given my clients pseudonyms in order to protect their identities.

Peter was exceptional, for most of my clients were quite verbal, even if they had difficulty describing feelings and other internal processes. As many were psychotic, I learned how to hear this other, more symbolic language. I became adept at reading symbols, whether drawn on a piece of paper or executed with a body. I enjoyed this way of thinking – allowing my thoughts to roam and associate, moving between images as well as lines. I learned to intersperse symbolic language with more logically determined thought, and to weave the two together in therapy. By tuning in to other senses and welcoming them into the whole, I was learning their language.

Once I understood, or thought I grasped, my clients' more primary process, symbolic language, I could act as a translator. By interpreting their communications I was teaching them secondary process thinking, a language they needed to learn in order to function more effectively in society. Even though they had grown up in America, they hadn't incorporated this language and were suffering from a kind of language disability.

One adolescent boy, Steven, had this type of problem. He had no distance from his feelings, and couldn't talk about them. He *was* the feeling. As his therapist, I aimed to help him develop a perspective on his feelings, get a handle on them, label them, so that he could begin to deal with them.

After Steven had been in therapy with me for a couple of years I accepted a position in another setting. We needed to say goodbye to each other. I knew that this would not be easy for Steven, and that he would be unable to let me know how difficult it was.

After our final session we walked down the corridor, as we had done on many other occasions. When we came to the bell for the fire alarm, Steven leaped into the air, extending his tall frame upwards, and managed to touch the bell with his hand. I recognized this as a form of communication. Assuming the role of translator, I made a comment, almost as an aside, about his being alarmed about my leaving. While he couldn't tell me with words, he'd managed to express what he needed to say.

I'm grateful to clients like Steven who helped me become more proficient at hearing symbolic language. When I began working with "healthier" clients who use language differently, I continued using this language to understand the processes underlying our work. My mind wanders and roams, associates, plays with symbols, taps into body sensations, leaps from one image to the next, and hears meanings inside meanings. My language disability is long forgotten – replaced by joyful excursions into worlds of inner meaning.

Words

Although therapists are often nicknamed "shrinks," I prefer to think of the work we do as having an expansive effect on clients. Rather than shrink capabilities, we enable clients to open inner doors, widen horizons, unfurl leaves, and develop hidden potentials. And we use words to facilitate this process.

Psychotherapy has been dubbed the talking cure. There is no laying on of hands, but a layering with words. We use words to communicate with the psyche.

Like most people, I never paid much attention to words. I took my words and those of others for granted, assuming that we were always talking about the same thing. Even after becoming a psychologist, I was sloppy with words. I used my own words when talking with clients, freely substituting my words for theirs. If someone spoke of feeling "mad" about something that had happened, I'd readily talk about their "angry" feeling. None of my training taught me how to use words skillfully, surgically.

I'm indebted to David Grove for showing me the importance of language. By teaching me to pay attention to words, he showed me how to use tools that I'd been haphazardly tossing around. I hadn't been paying attention to which tools I used when, for I'd been trying to address less conscious regions of the mind using secondary process language. By showing me ways of working with primary process language forms, metaphors, he taught me to differentiate between different tools – to use a rake for making adjustments to the surface of soil, and to use a spade whenever I wanted to go beneath the surface.

When I first attended one of David Grove's seminars, I was impressed with his mastery of language and his innovative use of metaphor. Rather than aiming to make the unconscious conscious by analyzing symbols, he works with the symbols themselves. Information that is enfolded in a symptom is explored symbolically, metaphorically. And while it has taken me a while to incorporate his ideas into my work, one of the first things he reminded me to do was pay attention to the fact that words have many meanings.

One glance at a dictionary demonstrates that most words have more than one meaning. While a word's denotative meaning is its literal translation, exact definition, its connotative meaning refers to its associative connections, other meanings that have become attached to the word. As these associative connections can be symbolic, therapists listen to these meanings whenever we want to understand a client's underlying process. By encouraging our minds to associate, play with symbols, and hear meanings behind meanings, we make interpretations, supply connections, help make the illogical logical. And even though we can get bogged down in the more masculine, interpretive mode, there are times when this approach is useful for clients.

Most therapy is conducted in more conscious regions of the psyche using secondary process language. This therapy addresses current concerns, interpersonal situations, and behavioral issues. While we may adhere to the denotative meanings of words, we also expand these meanings horizontally by paraphrasing clients' words, slightly shifting their meanings. By offering our thoughts and associations, we're sharing our perspective, another view to consider.

When we work with conscious processes we're helping clients make sense of their experiences. We ask "why" questions, directing clients to focus on reasons for their behavior, their motivation. This line of questioning encourages secondary process thinking, for it looks to explain behavior. Clients are relieved to discover the logic behind their seemingly illogical thoughts and irrational behavior.

If clients lack the interpersonal skills for building marriages, communicating with friends, or handling issues at work, we can teach them skills that are helpful in these situations. Clients learn to be better communicators by hearing how we use words. As I'm inclined to model the kind of behavior clients are trying to learn, I usually don't role play with them. Instead, I offer suggestions of what that client could say to his or her spouse, friend, lover, or employer. And while they may be disposed to try imitating me, I encourage them to find their own words – words that come to them naturally, feel right for them.

When discussing a difficulty one client, Sam, was having with his daughter, I suggested a way that he could set limits on her behavior. After offering my thoughts, Sam immediately responded: "Oh I could never say that!" to which I replied, "No, you wouldn't. Those are my words. What words could *you* use?" Knowing that practicing in the safety of my office would help prepare Sam for speaking with his daughter, I encouraged him to formulate the exact words he could use in that situation.

Clients bring up problems they have with their spouses, their children, their lovers, their bosses. Even if some of their problems are rooted in earlier, unresolved experiences, it is often helpful to explore the here-and-now situation, the current dilemma. And while these discussions are usually conducted in more conscious regions of the psyche, they frequently raise questions about underlying issues that could be contributing to the difficulty.

A 36-year-old woman came to see me because of difficulties with her boyfriend. Julie wanted to get married, to settle down and have a family, but she was involved with a man who seemed unable to make a commitment to marry her. They had previously parted for seven months, partially over the issue of marriage, and after pining away for each other had resumed their relationship. Even though Julie was feeling trapped by his indecision, she was afraid to break away from him because she had felt devastated the last time they separated.

Deciding to ask additional questions, I inquired about Julie's family and rapidly discovered that her father had died three years earlier. As we continued to talk, I heard a number of connections between her father's death and her current predicament. Julie's inability to separate from her boyfriend was a new experience, for prior to her father's death she had readily severed unsatisfactory relationships with men. Another clue came from the sequence and timing of events. She had met this boyfriend while her father was dying and her issues with the relationship seemed to climax every February, the month her father had died. Not only had they broken up in February, but here she was sitting in my office during another

February, struggling with the question of whether to sever this relationship.

I shared my observations with Julie, outlining various connections between her current relationship and unresolved issues about her father's death. It appeared as if her inability to let go of this man who was not giving her what she wanted was tied to her inability to let go of her father who, like her boyfriend, had also been detached and unavailable. And while she couldn't hold onto her father, she could keep holding onto a relationship with her boyfriend. She was unconsciously repeating a pattern that kept her tied to her father and let her avoid fully mourning his loss.

By sharing these observations, I was trying to help Julie make sense of her current predicament. When I finished, she looked at me with hope glistening through tear-filled eyes and asked, "Do you think that if I sort out my feelings about my father's death I'll be able to think more clearly about this particular relationship?" I told her that while I couldn't make any promises, I did feel it would be useful for her to work through her feelings about her father's death, and to see if she could separate her feelings about her father from her feelings about this man. Ending our first session on this hopeful note, she had a clear sense of the direction we would be taking together.

This entire session was spent talking in a rational, logical manner. While I made some interpretations and hypothesized about underlying, less conscious issues, I used secondary process language throughout the discussion, freely substituting my words for hers. When we ended the session, Julie's predicament made sense, and she felt better. But I knew that in order to mourn her father's loss and work through earlier unresolved issues with him, she might need to connect with deeper feelings of anger, sadness, loss, and despair. As this process would require her to sense, rather than make sense, I would need to use words capable of tapping into another language form.

To communicate with deeper regions of the psyche, the land of less conscious processes, it is necessary to use the form in which its information is stored. And while this language is symbolic language, many therapists persist in using secondary process language – psychological interpretations, logic. Interpretation can be useful when clients wish to understand something about themselves, but dissociated, dispossessed parts of the psyche don't speak this language. It isn't the language of clients' lost voices, their symptoms.

Clients bring us their symptoms, their lost voices. We need to speak a language that addresses these symptoms, a language they can hear. As lost voices have been banished from more conscious regions of the mind, we don't have direct access to them through linear thought. Their channels for communication are through the imagination and via the body.

Our bodies continually process information. In addition to the myriad self-regulatory processes that go on inside our bodies, various sense organs are continually receiving information from the outside world. Much of this goes on outside awareness.

Each of our senses provides an ongoing stream of information that we use to organize our experiences (Grinder & Bandler, 1976). We orient ourselves by seeing, smelling, touching, feeling, and tasting. Information from these, and any other senses currently clumped together using the word "intuition," is processed, and possibly stored, somatically. Preverbal memories are stored in these primary process language forms.

When we develop the use of words we have another form for processing and storing information. However, secondary process language doesn't replace the more basic primary process language. Our bodies continue processing and storing information somatically.

Sometimes our bodies store information that has been dispossessed by the self, banished from conscious regions of the mind. This happens when emotional material is too disturbing. It becomes dis-membered, cut off from the self. The information is stored in a part of the body, encapsulated in a symptom that keeps sending its message, trying to be heard.

Lost voices communicate through feelings, images, hunches, senses. This metaphorical language is symbolic language – a more feminine language with enfolded meaning, a language where "this" stands for "that," where "this" is "that." As lost voices speak in symbols, metaphors, the language of dreams, we need to be able to use language metaphorically, symbolically.

While I use art and other forms of symbolic expression with

clients, my medium is primarily words. Clients paint their internal
pictures with words. And they're not limited to the visual modality,
for words can sculpt a form, give texture, move, hear, connote
smells and tastes. Words are a pliable medium because they have
many levels of meaning.

If we want to reach into less conscious regions of the psyche, the
land of somatic experiences, we need to use words capable of
tapping into personal images, body sensations, sounds, smells, and
tastes. I, therefore, no longer paraphrase my clients' words when we
are addressing less conscious processes. There are often important
unconscious reasons behind the choice of a specific word.

Words are containers of information. They contain symbols, hidden meanings, inner pictures. The metaphors and symbols inside
clients' words are clues to a deeper underlying process. They are
the connotative meanings in those words.

When clients select a specific word, they are doing so for a
reason. If we substitute our word for theirs, we do them an injustice,
for we are altering their symbol, changing it in a significant way,
substituting our image for theirs. For example, if a client says she
feels depressed, "empty," we inadvertently change her connotative
meaning, alter the symbol within her word, if we take her word
literally and substitute the word "depleted." Instead of paraphrasing her word, expanding upon its literal meaning, we need to enter
into the symbolic world of "empty," to learn more about empty and
just what kind of empty that empty might be. In so doing we begin
moving into the metaphorical world, expanding the symbolic meaning of "empty."

David Grove offers a way of working with clients that enlarges
the meaning of a word by opening it up and extending its reach.
Instead of asking "why" questions, he suggests that we ask
"what," "when," "where," and "how" questions. While I'll be
giving a more detailed description of David's approach in a later
chapter on metaphor, it's basically a way of using words to access
primary process sensory language. It begins with asking clients to
locate their feelings, to recognize where they feel what they feel. It
involves becoming aware of the "where," focusing on where a
feeling is located, and what it's like when it's there. This line of
questioning serves to transform a nebulous idea such as "I'm 'de-

pressed' " into a more concrete, symbolic, somatic experience such as a "big empty hole in the stomach."

Words are the tools of our trade. We must use words artfully, select them according to the ongoing process, the territory in which we're travelling. At times we weave out – discuss relationships, pragmatic concerns, current issues. This is the land of secondary process, manifest content, logical rational words filled with denotative meanings, and definitions. At other times we weave in – plunging into the timeless depths of the psyche, unconscious symbolic regions, the land of images, pictures, kinesthetic sensations, latent content, and multiple meanings. Our words travel between different worlds, open inner channels, shift meanings, and glide from one language into another.

Trance

Psychotherapy is an inner journey, a voyage into hidden regions of the psyche. We travel through undeveloped land. This uncharted territory is inhabited by lost voices – disowned and dispossessed aspects of the self.

While there are no paved roads, no superhighways leading into less conscious regions of the mind, there seems to be a meandering path that moves in circles, spiralling in and out. I've been cutting through underbrush, trying to find this path, searching for avenues that could access clients' underlying processes. Along the way I became fascinated with hypnosis as a potential route into the unconscious.

The hypnotic tradition probably dates back to prehistoric times. "Primitive" cultures relied on various elements of the hypnotic process in their religious and healing practices. Healers of all denominations, shaman, witches, and priests, made use of hypnotic principles. Prior to the advent of the scientific method and the medicines it spawned, hypnotic principles were a primary tool for healing the sick.

Hypnosis isn't hocus-pocus or mumbo jumbo. While we don't know exactly how it works, it became recognized as a technique with scientific respectability in the late 1880s, only to fall into disrepute after Freud denounced its use. While political leaders, advertising executives, stage hypnotists, and cult leaders take advantage of hypnotic techniques, traditionally trained psychotherapists, like myself, tend to shy away from their use.

My curiosity about a group of psychological phenomena raised important questions that eventually pointed me in the direction of hypnosis. While I had been trained to devise research that would guard against the possibility of experimenter bias influencing test results, I became intrigued with the fact that this could actually happen. How does an experimenter unconsciously influence subjects to get desired experimental results? The placebo effect posed a similar question, for I wondered how sugar cubes could mimic the results of a powerful drug. And then there was the question of spontaneous remission. I couldn't dismiss it as being a statistical anomaly, due to chance, and I became curious about why it happened. How do some people recover from "incurable" diseases?

A few adventurous souls have been researching these and similar questions. They haven't found the answers, but their studies validate the body-mind connection and raise questions about how unconscious processes exert their influence throughout our systems. We now know that hardiness isn't purely a biological given, for attitudinal factors do affect the immune system and influence disease. And while we still don't know how it works, the placebo effect attests to the power of suggestion.

Still looking for answers, and hoping to learn ways of helping clients access their less conscious processes, I turned to hypnosis. I threw myself into learning as much as possible by attending a variety of conferences, seminars, and workshops. After gaining experience with different approaches, I realized that the term *hypnosis* covers a wide range of practices.

Despite differences in philosophy and style, hypnotic procedures follow a similar basic format. First, an altered state of consciousness, trance, is induced and deepened. While this hypnogogic or trance state can be healing in and of itself, its characteristic of heightened suggestibility is also used therapeutically. Different techniques are used, depending upon what the client is trying to accomplish – whether the client wants a specific behavioral change, such as smoking cessation, or whether the client is aiming for deep personality change where a technique such as age regression to recover a memory might be helpful. Hypnosis ends with the client returning to his or her usual state of awareness before leaving the office.

While major differences exist between various hypnotic approaches, most have to do with style. Classical hypnosis is more direct. Its formalized methods of induction and deepening are obvious to the client. Suggestions are also offered directly, with the therapist clearly telling the client what to do.

Indirect forms of hypnosis became popular through the work of

Milton Erikson. While he had a natural gift for inducing trance without using traditional induction techniques, his major contribution was his indirect style of making suggestions. They were embedded in stories or teaching tales.

While I was impressed with the power of hypnotic techniques, I shied away from using them in my practice. Something didn't feel right. At first I blamed this feeling on my inexperience. But after completing a series of seminars and training programs in both classical and indirect forms of hypnosis, I no longer felt inadequate or incompetent.

Thinking about my resistance to using hypnosis, I realized that I wasn't comfortable playing the masculine role of the powerful hypnotist. I didn't like the idea of telling someone what to do, inducing them to do it, when I was of the opinion that clients should be empowered by our work. Even the indirect method of telling stories relied too much on my own associations, which were often relevant to clients' difficulties, but were my associations, not theirs. Whenever I tried using hypnosis I felt as if I was performing psychological surgery on an anesthetized patient, cutting and suturing in the dark.

As I wanted clients to be actively involved in their healing, I stopped using hypnosis. But I didn't forget the training, for I noticed that clients frequently appeared to be in a trance; their eyes shifted aside and they stared off into space. While I'd previously recognized that clients were travelling inside themselves, wrapped up in their associative processes, I hadn't called this state "trance." I gradually realized that most therapists induce naturalistic trances by the kinds of questions we ask. With or without training in hypnosis, we learn to induce trance.

The process of therapy focuses on looking in, on listening to an internal voice. We ask clients questions about themselves – their feelings, their associations, their lives. In order to answer our questions they focus inside – finding the memory, the sensation, the idea, the words with which to respond to our inquiry. They're in a trance, an altered state of consciousness.

Trance is an integral part of every therapy. When I started watching clients carefully, I noticed them weaving in and out of trance. Sometimes the shift in consciousness is brief, a momentary excursion into inner space. At other times, they appear lost in reverie. If I stay quiet and still, allowing their thoughts to lead them where they need to go, they return to the room having made an inner connection.

The type of in-sight we aim for is obtained in trance. It isn't intellectual, but emotional – an inner feeling and seeing. Trance seem to facilitate the inner shifts that lead to psychological change.

The idea that entering an altered state of consciousness promotes psychological change is far from new. Ancient meditational techniques are still reputed to provide the road to enlightenment, to personal transformation. And while the mind-altering drugs of the 1960s were quick fixes, rapid ways of entering altered states of consciousness, today's fitness generation extols the extraordinary benefits of the runner's high. Whether we call the practice meditation, visualization, or hypnosis, we are making use of trance.

Whenever we are entranced, such as when meditating or in love, we seem to have access to a pool of inner resources that are unavailable during other times. These resources lie in an internal place, a space that taps into deeper regions of the mind, less conscious processes which include the healing power of nature.

Realizing that trance seems to play an important therapeutic role, I became excited about making a more conscious use of trance. While I'd been trained to ask questions and encourage associations, I'd never thought to do so with an eye toward inducing a trance. I decided to start using my tools of trance induction.

A well-phrased therapist question facilitates trance. Even the question "What did you have for breakfast?" invites trance. In order to answer the question, the client needs to leave the here and now, travel to another time and another place. Upon finding the answer, the client usually returns to the here and now and continues conversing with the therapist. This back-and-forth process is common during many conversations. But when people try to address deeply rooted, emotionally troubling issues, they usually need to explore their inner space and gain access to underlying processes. This is a time when principles of trance induction become useful.

Trance is induced by repetition and rhythm. While tribal practices of rhythmic chanting and drumming are still used throughout the world to induce altered states of consciousness, therapists don't rely on drums. We use our voices to create a similar effect by speaking rhythmically, repeating ourselves, and asking recursive questions.

I liken trance induction to rocking a baby to sleep. When a baby is upset and cranky, we take the baby into our arms and begin moving our bodies rhythmically, gently rocking back and forth. This motion usually has its intended effect, for the baby calms down and sometimes goes to sleep. Not only does the baby seem soothed by this motion, but we also feel calmer, more balanced, at peace. It's as if the rocking motion is built into our psyches.

Repetition and rhythm gently rock our conscious, vigilant minds to sleep. The mind is lulled into a sense of safety and it goes elsewhere. This isn't always based on a conscious assessment of safety, for we readily "space out" while driving a car. The sounds of tires repeatedly turning, and the sight of pavement constantly moving, exert a hypnotic effect. Our bodies automatically steer the car toward our destination, but our minds are travelling down internal pathways. We are surprised to find ourselves at our destination, for we don't remember having driven there.

When clients look to grapple with a lost part of their selves, we can use our voices to facilitate their inner journey. By using repetition and modulating our voices rhythmically, we can help them enter a dissociated state where they can more readily access dissociated parts of their selves. Their lost voices can begin to be heard.

Lost voices speak in symbols and metaphors, a more primary process somatic language. While I'll be talking about communicating with lost voices in the chapter on metaphor, it's important to keep in mind that lost voices don't live in conscious regions of the mind. They've been dissociated, relegated to the land of less conscious processes.

Dissociation is a defense mechanism that protects the psyche from traumatic experiences. While Freud and Breuer (1966) recognized the defensive nature of dissociation, and Sullivan (1940, 1953) clarified its integral role in ego development, we've only recently recognized it as a symptom of abuse.

People who have been physically abused learn to dissociate. In order to survive the abuse, they dissociate from it by separating from their bodies – leaving the body to experience the abuse while they, the conscious part of themselves, go elsewhere. As the memory for the experience may, thereby, be stored in the body, the conscious region of the mind cannot re-call the event. The event may appear forgotten, but it continues exerting its influence via the body. Psychosomatic symptoms and persistent nagging feelings can be wounded parts of ourselves that are crying out to be heard.

Rape, war, and ritualistic abuse are extreme examples of traumatic events. While their horror must never be minimized, we all experience some trauma in our lives; it's inherent in development, part of growing up. We survive the trauma by dissociating – separating ourselves from a part of ourselves – from the object of scrutiny, the source of pain, the seed of difficulty. These wounded parts never truly heal, for they're protected by bandages, hidden from sight. But their lost voices keep asking to be heard – to be re-membered, re-connected with the self.

Some therapists tend to correct clients when they talk about their experiences in a dissociated way. And while I used to see my task as always helping clients to own their experiences, I now recognize that dissociation can help some clients connect with earlier, traumatic events. Instead of working against the dissociation, we may need to encourage it. The dissociated state can protect clients, help them survive the pain.

As hypnotic techniques encourage dissociation, they are a useful therapeutic tool. However, they have their time and place. I vary my style according to where a client is travelling. My language shifts. My tone switches. My entire therapeutic demeanor varies with the ongoing process.

When dealing with the here and now, addressing aspects of "reality" or interpersonal issues, I generally look at a client and maintain eye contact. In addition, I tend to speak directly, more matter-of-factly. But when clients look to journey inside themselves, it's best to limit external distractions. This includes me. I take myself out of their picture by averting my eyes and looking elsewhere. I also use my voice to encourage the internal shift, the focusing inward. I speak slowly, softly, and rhythmically. My words repeat themselves, forming recursive questions.

My client and I generally sit in two reclining swivel chairs. Although the client is usually positioned so we face one another, the chairs easily move in other directions. Many clients reposition their chair whenever they begin focusing inside themselves. While a few tilt the chair backwards and close their eyes, others remain upright and shift slightly aside. Some prefer to sit on the couch. They too shift their eyes, stare into space, or close their eyes when they're travelling inside.

One client, Sarah, decided to vary where and how she sits in my office according to the direction she wishes to take. After many months of sitting in a chair, Sarah asked if she could move to the couch. As I encouraged her to sit wherever she wished, Sarah went over to the couch and positioned herself so that she could look out the window rather than at me. In addition, she decided to lie down, propping her head up with a few assorted pillows I leave there.

Since then, Sarah often walks into the room and heads straight for the couch. At other times she sits in the chair. According to Sarah, she sits in the chair when she wants to connect with me while talking about her issues. This happens when she wants to tell me about some events in her life, but doesn't want to "get into them," only let me "know about them." As she wants to understand her situation and is looking for another perspective, I'll offer a suggestion or make an interpretation.

When Sarah is "on the couch," we work in a more symbolic fashion. I stay out of her vision, and my language addresses her metaphors, inviting them to communicate their meanings and share their information. According to Sarah, she goes "someplace else" in a "bubble, flying around." She hears my voice but I, her therapist, am no longer there. Only my voice travels with her.

Although Sarah never read Freud and had never heard of free association, she chose to lie on the couch. She sensed that my couch would be her magic carpet. It would help her travel where she needed to go – into the land of secondary processes – the realm of hidden meanings and lost connections.

Trance is a dissociated state. While it's an inner womb that provides a sense of safety, a feeling of security, it's also an inroad, a path into ourselves. It helps tap into the vast reservoir of nature's healing resources and give birth to the missing pieces – the stunted lost parts of our selves.

Entering into a trance is moving into sacred space. It's neither here nor there, but between – between conscious and unconscious, between right brain and left brain, between masculine and feminine, between mind and body. It's a path for gaining access, an entry zone.

Metaphor

Meta means to change, to transform, and that's exactly what metaphors do in our work. These bubbles from the unconscious are vessels, containers of information, that hold keys to unlocking inner doors and releasing imprisoned parts of the psyche. Metaphors contain seeds for healing.

Until I learned how to work with metaphors I felt frustrated and stuck. My clients seemed to benefit from therapy, but I wasn't satisfied. Sometimes an interpretation seemed to click, but helping clients understand their difficulties didn't necessarily lead to change, and I wondered if there were another way of addressing less conscious processes. While I was making connections, offering interpretations, and helping make the illogical logical, I yearned to be capable of also exploring the illogical, the irrational, the symbolic. Instead of only acting as a translator, I wanted the option of speaking the language, talking with symbols, encouraging their form of communication.

I first heard about metaphors in an English class. I learned that it is a symbol, a word or phrase that stands for something else. It is used by poets and other writers to expand a word beyond its literal meaning. By having "this," stand for "that," a writer suggests images, feelings, sounds, and other sensory experiences that embellish upon the meaning of a word and give life to an idea. Thus John Donne speaks to us on many levels when he says, "No man is an island, entire of itself; every man is a piece of the continent, a part of the main" (Donne, 1624/1961, p. 467). His geographic references travel below the surface of our conscious minds and touch us on a deeper, more somatic, level. We feel connected, not only to fellow human beings, but also to the earth, this planet.

Becoming a psychologist expanded my understanding of metaphor. I saw how cultural metaphors, in the form of myths and fairy tales, are teaching tales. They bypass conscious regions of the mind, which tend to focus on literal meanings, reach further into our psyches, and indoctrinate us into the ways of our culture. Sitting safely on a parent's lap, we're transported into worlds of goblins and gremlins, pigs and wolves, "Goldilocks and the Three Bears." These lessons about good and bad, right and wrong, become permanently etched inside our psyches.

Since myths are cultural metaphors they also reflect the psychological makeup of an era. Sigmund Freud saw the Oedipal myth as reflecting a universal human experience and, therefore, used it to explain psychological phenomena. His interpretation of this myth formed the basis for his theory of human development and the structure of the human psyche.

When I became a psychotherapist my interpretations of poems expanded into other arenas. Using all of my senses I tried to interpret clients' feelings in terms of the underlying meaning, the latent content, the message being sent. I helped clients hear the messages in their dreams by listening to my own associations and "gut" reactions. By helping them listen to less conscious parts of themselves I was acting as a translator, a go-between, and I couldn't help feeling that something was lost in this process. It was like being limited to only reading the subtitles of a foreign movie. Without pictures, sounds, and other innuendos of meaning, something important is missing – the magical part, the poetic art.

Milton Erikson discovered part of this missing piece when he began telling stories to his clients. His stories acted like fairy tales, for they contained messages that reverberated through the psyche, influencing unconscious emotions and attitudes. This approach worked for Erikson, and it attests to the healing power of stories, anecdotes, and tasks with metaphorical meaning. But, as I've mentioned before, I'm not totally comfortable with this approach because the metaphor, or story, is constructed by the therapist, not the client. While the therapist may be tuned into a client's underlying issues, the metaphor contains the therapist's associations and uses his or her own words. It too readily reflects the therapist's feelings.

When constructing metaphors, therapists may follow guidelines such as those outlined by David Gordon (1978) or Philip Barker (1985). However, when we sit in our offices, listening to clients, we're human beings, not analytical machines. Our words are influenced by our own unique ways of experiencing events – our somatic experiences, our feelings. And feelings, in and of themselves, are a form of communication.

I believe that therapy is basically about healing hurt feelings. These feelings are people's symptoms, their troublesome feelings. And contrary to how some people describe their symptoms, feelings don't come out of the blue or float around in the mind.

Feelings are body sensations, somatic forms of communication, messages from the body. If we've been working too hard, we may feel tired; if our bodies want some energy (food), we may feel hungry; and if we receive some upsetting news we may feel sad and distraught, as if we've been punched in the stomach.

While it's important to listen to feelings and hear their messages, most of us don't know how to hear the language of feelings because they speak a metaphorical language. We've been trained to trust the literal use of words and stick to logical explanations. But if we want to hear what a feeling is trying to tell us, we need to stop asking "why" questions and try another line of inquiry. We need to speak their language.

Some feelings are messages from disowned and dispossessed parts of the psyche. These messages keep repeating themselves over and over and over again. They're our clients' symptoms and they contain the lost voices I've talked about in earlier chapters. And as lost voices communicate in feelings or somatic sensations, a metaphorical language, the task of the therapist is to help clients translate their troublesome feelings into metaphors. According to David Grove, this requires that we avoid contaminating clients' metaphors with our own associations and meanings. Instead, he offers a method of inquiry that helps clients discover their own metaphors and create their own teaching tales.

If a client were to come to David Grove saying, "I'm depressed," he would respond by asking "And when you're depressed, how do you know you're depressed, when you're depressed?" Notice the recursiveness of this question; the same phrase is used at the beginning and end. This helps a client turn his or her attention around and begin focusing inside. After pondering the question for a while, the client might talk about depression, and then describe a feeling such as "I've been feeling tired."

Once the client identifies a feeling, Grove recommends switching to asking "where" questions such as: "And as you've been feeling tired, where have you been feeling tired, when you've been feeling tired." This question helps ground a feeling in the body. And because people generally aren't accustomed to paying attention to where they feel what they feel, it usually takes a sequence of "where" questions to determine a feeling's specific location.

Continuing with our example, the client might respond with a statement such as "I feel tired all over," to which Grove might respond by asking "And when you feel tired all over, where do you feel tired all over, when you feel tired all over. Is tired all over inside or outside your body?" And if the client responds with "It's inside," Grove would help the client further refine the location by asking questions such as "And when it's inside, is it more above your waist or below your waist, when it's inside?" Usually the client eventually focuses on a specific area such as "It's in my heart."

When asking these questions it's important to use the client's exact words. Even the slightest change in wording can entirely shift the client's meaning. This includes using the same verb tense, for clients sometimes switch to the past tense when accessing memories from the past. And if the client starts referring to "it," as in the example above, the therapist would also switch and begin asking questions about "it."

Sometimes clients don't answer with words. They identify an area of their body by pointing to it, touching it, or moving their hand around a particular spot. This can happen for many reasons. Sometimes they don't have a name for the location, particularly if they've regressed to an earlier age and are accessing a memory that preceded their knowledge of the word for that area. It can also be because they're in a trance and it takes too much conscious effort to find the word. Regardless of the reason, it's important to stay with their process. As they haven't offered a word, the location shouldn't be given a name. Instead, the location can be referred to as "there."

Once a specific location is identified, Grove suggests switching into a "what" question such as "And as it's there, what's it like when it's there?" While this question is an open-ended question, some clients immediately produce detailed answers. Others have more difficulty, and it then becomes necessary to ask a series of questions designed to elicit a metaphor. These questions ask for specific sensory information. They can be asked as separate questions or combined into one sentence, leaving long pauses between the different types of information. Returning to the example I was using earlier, the therapist could ask, "And as it's in heart does it have a shape? . . . a size ? . . . a color? . . . texture? . . . any movement? . . . What's it like when it's in heart? And is there anything else?" If it looks as if the client is having difficulty answering these questions, he or she usually needs additional time. A statement such as "And take some time to get to know just what it's like when it's in heart" gives clients the permission they may need.

Once the initial feeling has been translated into its metaphorical equivalent, it is possible to begin having a conversation with "it." Let's say that our client answered our "What's it like?" questions with "Well, it's round, and dark, like a big empty hole." Using Grove's format, our next questions would be addressed to "big empty hole." We might ask a question such as "And what does 'big empty hole' want to have happen?" or "What does 'big empty hole' want to do?" These questions are followed by asking, "And how can that happen?" "And what would need to happen so that that can happen?" "And just when can that begin to happen?" These questions empower the lost voice that has been hidden inside the client's symptom – the big empty hole, the tiredness, the depression. Once it has an opportunity to be heard, it can begin to move. It can have something happen.

Once the metaphor begins moving, other changes usually follow. These shifts are assisted by asking the question: "And what happens next?" Before long the client is telling a metaphorical story, his or her own teaching tale.

David Grove's questions often help transform a troublesome feeling, something a client wants to get rid of, into something that can be listened to, heard, and used. As it is no longer a lost voice, it is free to contribute to the individual's well-being.

Like Milton Erikson, David Grove makes use of the naturalistic trance. Having attended many of his seminars, I can attest to the fact that his tone of voice, rhythmic way of speaking, and use of repetition have a hypnotic quality. But even without the help of these traditionally hypnotic tools, the questions themselves have the power to induce a hypnotic state.

As I'm neither Milton Erikson nor David Grove, I've had to search for my own style of using metaphors. While I'm more comfortable with Grove's questions because they encourage clients to create their own metaphors and teaching tales, they are merely a tool, a useful format, a helpful way of thinking about metaphors. They've taught me to be scrupulous with language and to stubbornly stick to clients' words whenever we're exploring less conscious processes.

I find that I need to feel my way with each client, trying this and that, as we go on our journey together. There are no pat formulas for working with metaphors, but sometimes a few well-timed questions can yield helpful information. This was the case with Jessica, who had been using her therapy to focus on anger and depression when she mentioned another troublesome feeling. She described herself as a "doing rather than a being person" and mentioned that she feels "tension from stuff that has to be done." In a session soon afterwards, she refined this sensation as feeling "driven." As it was the end of our session, I decided not to explore "driven" immediately. Instead, I suggested that she might get to know "driven," find out as much as possible about "driven," where "driven" was located, and what "driven" was like. I also added that she might want to write this information down sometime during the week and that we could use it during our next session.

We began our next session with Jessica reading from a notebook. After describing "driven" as a "coiled, rigid spring" located in her "top part," she spent some time talking about what the feeling itself was like and then spoke about a dream she felt was related to this issue. As discussing this information took practically the whole session, there wasn't enough time to explore her metaphor. But I did suggest that we might find out more about "driven" by getting to know the "coiled, rigid spring" during our next session.

Our next session began with Jessica talking about her "blatant anxiety." It wasn't long before "driven" and "coiled spring" came up. Speaking softly and rhythmically, I began asking Grove's questions, starting with "where." She described "coiled spring" as located in the area from her "waist down to knees" and that it was "curved to fit my body."

When Jessica definitely knew where "coiled spring" was located, I began a series of questions inquiring about its various attributes. I asked about its shape, size, color, texture, and whether there was anything else. Jessica described "coiled spring" as "grey . . . steel . . . hard, thin, bigger than wire . . . heavy duty, very, very strong . . . always ready to move." As her last statement indicated that she was ready to move on to the next question, I asked about what "coiled spring" might want to do. She spent some time talking about how the spring wanted to "become straight," and recalled a memory from first grade, describing what it was like to go from a "house with people who did things" to school where she was required to sit still. Continuing to focus on "coiled spring" she recognized that "coiled spring wants to leave," and then went on to say, "It's trying to help me get out of situations that are too much." By the end of the session Jessica felt differently about "coiled spring." She saw it as belonging to her, and decided to begin listening to it, rather than fight it.

While this was not the end of Jessica's therapy, she started feeling differently about messages from her body that she had previously labelled as "tension." Her metaphor of "coiled spring" was initially something she battled, but it also contained a seed for healing. She could now hear the lost voice that had been calling to her in the form of "coiled spring." And by paying attention to what "coiled spring" was telling her, she resumed growing.

The process I've been describing may sound easy, but there are never simple solutions to clients' difficulties. Sometimes metaphorical questions hit stone walls, and then I know to try a different direction. What works in one session may not work in the next. As in my garden, I keep checking the soil, using all of my senses to determine what might be helpful at the time.

Every gardener knows that timing is important. We keep watching the soil and feeling its texture, looking for clues about what to do when. Sometimes we water, at other times we mulch. Metaphors are one of this gardener's many tools.

Using metaphors in psychotherapy requires a playful openness to language, a willingness to welcome images and sensations, to catch a symbol as it goes flying by, then holding it, embracing it, and beginning a conversation with it. This is the art of therapy. It involves using the poetry in words to breathe life into petrified forests. And as no man, or woman, is an island, our metaphors tap into the main.

Creativity

Masculine and feminine come together in the act of creation. Their dancing and weaving become a momentary whole out of which a new life is formed – a seed, a new beginning. If this seed is nurtured, it begins to grow, sending roots into Mother Earth and arms towards Father Sky.

While I've always known that creation is a continual process, I never really knew what this meant until I started composting. Making compost taught me that there is no such thing as life or death. Life is the continual process of creation.

Nothing is more life-giving to a garden than compost. It nourishes the soil with organic matter, providing nutrients that are readily available to the next generation of plants. If a plant is ever in difficulty, struggling to survive, compost will help it revive, get a grip on life. And while compost has these life-giving and life-saving properties, it is also a product of the natural decaying process. In this respect, it is full of death.

Gardeners make compost by saving everything from kitchen scraps to weeds culled from the garden with soil on their feet. While my neighbors toss leftovers and peelings down garbage disposals or into trash cans, I'm busy saving mine. All these "waste materials" go into an ever ready container. By the time I have a chance to carry the contents of this container outside, it has usually begun to decompose. It becomes a disgusting, malodorous mess – slimy and unappetizing, to say the least.

This smelly rotten mess is gingerly escorted outside, usually at arm's length, and unceremoniously dumped onto an awaiting pile. All sorts of substances are added to this pile, usually in haphazard order. Adding as many different ingredients as possible creates the essential mix of varied material. Whenever we clean out the chicken coop, rotting woodshavings, replete with urine and manure, are dumped on the pile. Weeds, leaves, or grass clippings – the pile doesn't discriminate. It accepts everything but plastic and other inorganic substances.

When this pile becomes a large heap, it is time to start the next. During the heat of summer, adding water helps speed the decaying process. Then all the pile needs is time. Decomposition generates heat that fuels the inner fires. Gradually the pile shrinks in size, cools, and miraculously becomes loose, friable, rich earth.

Until I began making compost I thought of life and death as two finite states. I wanted to hold onto life and avoid death. Making compost taught me that life and death, creation and destruction, are all part of the same whole. The lines can't be cleanly drawn, for it's difficult to tell where one ends and the other begins. Life and death are part of each other. Nature doesn't operate according to the either/or principle.

Instead of thinking of creation and destruction as being separate entities, I began thinking of them, and other seemingly contradictory states, in terms of a wheel that's in perpetual motion, turning, moving from one to the other, blurring all distinctions. Complementary elements, positioned opposite one another around the periphery, balance the wheel. This is the wheel of nature – our constant moving force.

Nothing is static, but ever moving, flowing, in flux. Beginnings and endings, creation and destruction, birth and death, connection and separation are woven together. They are the whole of life. And nature's creative thread ties it all together.

In nature there is no such thing as inactivity or inertness. As in my compost pile, "dead" matter continues to grow. After leaves, branches, and other "dead" materials fall to the ground, nature's composting process goes to work. Old, used-up, dried-out, and otherwise "dead" substances gradually become loose, viable earth that is full of nutrients, full of life. Growing is healing.

But sometimes growth is impeded. When our inner earth is frozen or compacted, the composting process is interrupted. Parts of us become stunted. We get stuck in unproductive, repetitive patterns. Instead of growing, or moving ahead in spirals, we keep going round and around the same circle.

I suspect it's no accident that the word "unbalanced" has come to mean crazy, insane. If a part of us is prevented from growing, we become unbalanced. In the psychological arena, this happens when a potentially balancing aspect of the self is suppressed or disowned. The psyche becomes unbalanced.

Psychotherapists generally recognize that psychological difficulties stem from imbalances within the psyche. And as any one-sidedness can be a clue to a potentially denied or disowned aspect of the self, we often address the one-sidedness by paying attention to the complementary aspect. In helping clients recognize their conflicts, their ambivalence, we're contributing to their compost by identifying a balancing aspect, the complementary feature that completes their whole.

Most psychotherapists are trained to look for missing aspects of polarities. Early in my career I learned that sad, depressed people are often also angry. They frequently have underlying anger or rage that has been denied, avoided, suppressed, or otherwise cut off from their experience. As anger can be freeing and energizing, I was taught to help such a person recognize this other facet by first naming this potential feeling, wondering out loud whether he or she may also feel angry.

On the other hand, a person who appears overly angry and hostile is often also sad. This person may characteristically respond to psychological hurts with anger and outrage, but doesn't allow himself or herself to acknowledge the sad, pained, hurt feelings that have occurred. When working with these people we search to find, and then name, the sad feelings.

While it's recognized that imbalances need to be righted in order for healing to occur, talking about imbalances doesn't necessarily lead to change. Something else needs to happen, but none of my training taught me how to translate the compost-making process into practices that would help clients rebuild the soil within themselves. I had to learn that myself.

After living on Harmony Farm for quite a while I started noticing that I was feeling different. Where before I had been searching, always looking for something, now I was feeling whole, more complete. And while I knew that something had shifted, I didn't understand what had happened.

Wanting to comprehend this change, make sense of what was happening inside, I decided to start writing a journal. As I began finding words for my experience, I started noticing that when I'm out with nature, cradled in her arms, I feel her rhythms, her cycles, her creative dance. Her balance seeps in, becomes part of my being, enabling me to become balanced within my self.

Nature helped me connect with missing aspects of my self, my lost parts. Even after recognizing this process, I still couldn't identify how internal shifts take place – what actually sets them off. This unanswered question began haunting me. It was fundamental to my work.

As the school of natural healing is in my backyard, I continued attending daily classes by taking walks in the woods and keeping all my senses tuned into nature's ways. I allowed my mind to wander and roam, and when ideas began germinating I wrote them down. At first my thoughts went round and around. They were hazy, incomplete.

After a while I began feeling that the answer was within my reach. I sensed it, felt it, knew it. But I couldn't describe it. As I couldn't put it into words, I felt stuck in a quagmire, caught in an abyss between knowing and not knowing. I felt tense and uptight.

Although my tension kept mounting, I kept on writing, meddling with words, until something inexplicable happened. I took a breath and seemed to enter another space. It was no longer an abyss, it was more like a clearing. As if fog had been blown away by the in-breath, in the space, the pause before the out-breath, it all came clear. Like a bolt of lightning from the blue, it fell into place. I knew! The word was "tension."

Even though I'd always thought of tension in negative terms, it now had a positive side. I knew that the push for growth comes from tension. To be more specific, it comes from the dynamic taking place between opposites, from their interaction inside the compost pile. In my case, the tension came from the dynamic between knowing and not knowing. And nature's healing influence, her balancing process, is the unfolding tension between masculine and feminine – her creative dance.

It isn't enough for opposites to exist side by side, for then there is no tension, no dynamism between them. The dynamic of growth is produced by the interplay between different, contrasting elements.

The tension between them is the creative spark that ignites transformation.

But tension alone isn't enough. Its electricity leaps from pole to pole and needs a wire for travelling, a path to follow. While tension can mount, it can't grow without creativity. It needs a way of travelling, a vehicle.

Writing fueled my inner fires, and led me where I needed to go. As it gave me a way of connecting knowing with not knowing, I began wondering whether clients might also benefit from using a creative vehicle for their composting process. And even though none of my training ever addressed the issue of working with clients' creativity to facilitate growth, I began thinking that creative activities could be another tool for communicating with a lost voice.

Creative activities are a way of tuning in and listening to lost parts of ourselves. As they are vehicles for travelling inward, they give us a way of exploring abandoned regions of the psyche. The parts of ourselves that have been hurt, wounded, lost, and dispossessed are given a voice. Their messages are given a form, their intent expressed. Artistic productions are metaphors. They're a tool for communicating with lost, dispossessed parts of ourselves – our lost voices.

There are many vehicles for the creative process. While we're more familiar with arts such as painting, sculpting, photography, and writing, any activity that expresses something from inside ourselves can embody the creative process. These activities require a receptive attitude – opening to inner space without deciding what is to happen. Receptivity involves welcoming inner shifts, movement, and allowing the movement to travel where it wants to go, not where the person thinks it should move.

Creative vehicles don't travel in straight lines. In making connections they appear to weave, travelling back and forth from one pole to another. They give feeling a form – linking inside with outside, masculine with feminine, mind with body, primary with secondary process thinking, and right brain with left. This process is like making compost. It promotes balance, movement towards wholeness.

Recognizing the importance of creative vehicles, I decided to start incorporating them into my work with clients. While I never give assignments or prescribe such activities, I do encourage them. I support anything that involves receptivity, opening to inner space. As always, I listen carefully to clients, waiting for a clue that might lead to an undiscovered vehicle for travelling through dissociated regions of the psyche, their undeveloped land.

Sometimes it takes one session, other times months, even years, but each person does have a vehicle he or she can use. I help clients recognize their vehicles, know that they're there, and learn to trust them. Once they're familiar with a vehicle, I encourage them to use it. And as they travel down their paths, I help them recognize the signposts, learn to follow their signs.

While some therapists rely on creative vehicles during sessions, I tend to encourage clients to use this tool when they're by themselves. I suggest that clients write down associations they have between sessions, or draw pictures of something they're trying to describe. Sometimes they'll bring in material from home – a picture they've drawn, a poem they've written, or a form they've constructed. One client brought in a contraption made of twigs and string because it was the only way she could describe a particular feeling.

Many of my clients use music. While some are proficient at playing an instrument, others listen or sing. A number of clients write as the spirit moves them. They keep journals and pen poems, fairy tales, and parables. Baking bread is one person's vehicle, whereas another creates cakes. My clients weave baskets, rearrange rooms, and dig in wildflower gardens. And since both walking and meditating can also promote inspiration, many of my clients engage in one of these solitary activities.

Although clients frequently look to me to steer them where they need to go, I usually encourage them to learn how to use their own vehicles. Since I'm more of a gardener, I avoid becoming a pilot, but I do help them navigate through their journeys' twists and turns. Part of my role is to help each of them find a form of transportation they can use, and one person's vehicle may not be suited to another's inner terrain.

Whether I'm in my office or garden, I keep adding material to the compost pile. The "old" never goes away, but given the heat of time and the tension between opposites, the spark of life can regenerate growth. Nature took me by the hand and taught me to hear music playing between opposites. I aspire to use this aspect of nature's healing influence – to help clients weave back and forth between their opposites of masculine and feminine, linear and circular, rational and irrational, active and passive. I encourage the creative spark that leaps across poles – intertwining opposites.

The creative process entails giving form to a sense, a feeling, an idea. As a key to growth it can unlock inner doors, make connections, and solve inner dilemmas. When clients become artists they have tools for activating their own compost and fertilizing their inner lives.

Re-Membering

Symptoms contain lost voices that belong to wounded, disso-ciated, dispossessed aspects of the self. These lost voices have been dis-membered, separated off from the self, usually as a result of trauma – an event, or series of events, that were too overwhelming for the psyche to assimilate at the time.

Hurt, disowned, and dispossessed aspects of the self struggle to survive. While they may have been banished from the self, they make their presence felt in a variety of ways. They may appear as visual images, unwelcome thoughts, or memories that keep intrud-ing into consciousness. Sometimes they produce behavior such as compulsive activities or ritualistic acts. They can also exert their influence through feelings or sensations that keep repeating them-selves, refusing to go away. And while some of these feelings and sensations may be more psychological, others appear to be physical. Lost voices often use psychosomatic symptoms as their mouth-piece. They are asking to be heard.

Healing inner wounds involves repairing the psyche. When the self has been split asunder, it may need professional help in order to restore its unity. And even though psychotherapists can't mend torn psyches with a needle and thread, we can help people recover dis-membered aspects of their selves.

Psychotherapy is, in some ways, a re-membering process. It is a process of making connections, of listening to symptoms and hear-ing what they have to say. And while we aim to hear the meanings behind many types of symptoms, lost voices frequently take up residence in the body. It is, therefore, useful to pay attention to physiological processes and help clients hear their bodies' mes-sages.

Important differences notwithstanding, physical and psychologi-cal processes are inexorably intertwined. Nevertheless, as psycho-therapists primarily attend to the psyche, we are trained to see feelings as mental events. Most psychotherapists ask clients what they are feeling and then proceed to talk about the feeling – aiming to clarify it, shed light on it, and help understand it. These psychotherapists address feelings as if they were dissociated states, floating around in the mind, disconnected from the body. By focusing on the mind, and acting as if it exists independently of the body, they perpetuate the Cartesian mind-body split. They inadvertently dissociate the mind from the body and value the masculine mind, over the feminine body.

Although the healing arts have been divided into different departments, health practitioners need to pay attention to the whole person, the body as well as the mind. When working with clients we can affirm interconnection by helping them build the necessary bridges between their physical and psychological systems. One important way to do this is by asking clients where their feelings are located. Feelings often reside in particular body sites. We can also address other aspects of their physical well-being.

Psychotherapists should inquire about specific physical symptoms as well as clients' exercise, eating, and sleeping habits. While we must be careful not to medically diagnose and treat physical symptoms, we can take note of their psychological equivalence and offer suggestions as to how clients might take better care of their bodies. I like to let clients know that their physical states affect other aspects of their lives.

Whenever a client reports feeling anxious, I inquire about his or her diet, especially the intake of sugar, alcohol, and caffeine. These products stimulate the adrenal glands to increase physiological arousal, which is often experienced as anxiety. In addition to recommending that clients avoid using these stimulants, I teach them ways of relaxing their bodies, and encourage exercise.

Unless it's overdone, exercise is generally a health-promoting activity. It tones muscles, increases oxygen intake, and promotes general detoxification. Moreover, there are psychological benefits from exercise. One of these benefits is that exercise encourages us to communicate with our bodies.

Many clients are disconnected from their bodies. They don't know how to listen to their senses and hear what their bodies are telling them. Physical activity helps them pay attention to these messages and relate to their physical selves.

Some forms of exercise have additional benefits. Aerobic activities like dancing, running, walking, and swimming are natural antidepressants. These activities also release tension and thereby reduce anxiety. They promote psychological as well as physical well-being.

The last thing depressed clients feel like doing is exercising, but it is often very helpful for them. I remember one client, Alice, who was suicidal when she first came to see me. As she was severely depressed, we discussed the possibility of a referral for antidepressant medication. Although antidepressants had helped her once before, she was hesitant to begin taking them again. When I told her that exercise alleviates some of the physical aspects of depression, she mentioned that she used to run regularly but had stopped. After Alice resumed running, her depression began lifting. She mobilized energy to work on the issues that were responsible for her depression.

If clients are interested in trying a form of physical activity, it's essential that they do this for themselves, not to please their therapists, or anyone else. While clients may initially follow therapists' recommendations, unless they experience some value for themselves, they will soon drop the activities. They need to select activities that will fit into their lifestyles and suit their particular bodies. I encourage them to listen to their bodies, hear what they want, and learn to answer their requests.

When clients start listening to their bodies, they sometimes begin connecting with dissociated parts of their selves. If a traumatic experience has been banished from conscious regions of the mind, information about the experience is relegated to the land of less conscious processes. While the memory of the trauma becomes less accessible to verbal processes and linear logical thought, it can be encoded in somatic language.

Psychological trauma that is encoded in somatic language is often stored in body sites where it makes its presence felt in the form of psychosomatic symptoms. An experience can be replicated as a visual image, a sound, a smell, an emotional feeling, or a physical sensation. It can be retained in fragments or as a whole.

We are all amnesic for portions of our lives. As far as I know, these gaps in memory do not necessarily suggest the existence of forgotten traumatic experiences. However, clients start therapy because they're troubled by symptoms – feelings or behaviors that are causing them difficulty. Their symptoms often express dis-membered parts of the self – lost voices seeking to be re-membered.

Symptoms serve a purpose. They are there for a reason, usually because they have a story to tell. They narrate their story using symbolic language – a language of pictures and sounds, smells and tastes, feelings and sensations, images and ideas. Clients connect with the lost parts of their selves by listening to their symptoms, following associations, and hearing the underlying meanings. Mind and body cooperate in this re-membering process.

While I believe that it is not necessary for clients to relive the traumatic events in their lives, memories of unassimilated trauma often surface during psychotherapy. Exploring feelings can bring these previously suppressed memories to conscious awareness. Sometimes the recalled event is an experience the client never discussed with anyone. It remained undigested, raw in the psyche. Psychotherapy helps heal the wounds associated with these memories.

Psychotherapy can become pretty tricky with clients who have experienced extreme, repetitive, ritualistic abuse. These clients may begin therapy with no knowledge of such events in their lives. But as therapy progresses they may start having flashbacks. They become haunted by an earlier experience (or experiences); it descends upon them, intrudes into consciousness throughout the day. Sometimes they feel compelled to relive the experience or to abreact. While we must use all of our skills to modulate this process and keep clients from harming themselves or others, they may require the additional protection of psychotropic medication or hospitalization.

Many therapists are now seeing people with post-traumatic stress disorders. Dissociation is a typical defense of people who have had a traumatic experience, such as abuse. These people separate aspects of their experience (behavior, affect, sensation, and knowledge) in order to survive it (Braun, 1988a, 1988b). For example, they not only frequently separate themselves from the memory of the abuse, they also separate from their bodies during the abuse. They endure the abuse by not being fully there – by separating off the parts of the self that have to be there, while the rest of the self goes someplace else.

Although people who report experiences of being outside their bodies have often been subjected to some form of abuse, there are degrees of dissociation. Many clients describe occasions when they don't feel fully present in their bodies. For example, people with eating disorders talk about feeling as if "something else takes over," as if their hands have minds of their own when they reach for food. Panic attacks are often described in a similar way.

As I discussed in the chapter on stunting, dissociation is inherent in development; it is a natural part of growing up. However, growth is impeded, sometimes even stopped, when essential aspects of the self are disowned. Psychotherapy then aims to heal the wounds caused by these inner rifts. As therapists, our role is to help people engage with the lost parts of their selves.

As re-membering entails attending to the body and hearing its messages, I frequently ask clients where they feel what they feel. On one such occasion, I was working with a woman, Nancy, who had recently started therapy with me. Although she was primarily concerned about her husband's relationship with another woman, she recognized that they had both contributed to their marital difficulty.

As Nancy was aware that her tendency to be impatient, intolerant, and judgmental had put a barrier between herself and her husband, she was trying to find a different way of being with him. Talking about her difficulty dealing with ambiguity led us to a feeling, "angry." Responding to my "where" questions, Nancy stated that the feeling was "inside . . . throat . . . suffocated." Again I asked a "where" question, and Nancy responded, "back of my throat . . . strangulation." While exploring "strangulation," Nancy described a hand. I asked whether there was one or two hands. Nancy clearly identified "one." My next question was whether the hand was a left or a right hand. Again, Nancy knew. It was a right hand.

Although our hour was almost over, I wanted to see if Nancy could continue with this line of exploration. I took a risk by asking another question, "And hand is on throat . . . it's one hand . . . a right hand . . . and how old are you when right hand is on throat?" Nancy answered "three years old," confirming my suspicion that she was accessing a memory. However, our time was up. After mentioning that we needed to end our session, and making sure that it was "all right with three" to continue our discussion next time, I gave Nancy some time to reorient to the here and now. We then briefly chatted about the material that had surfaced.

When Nancy came in for her next appointment she shared the memory of what had happened when she was three and a half. Her mother was furious with her for having made a necklace out of bubblegum and had rubbed it off "very hard" with fluid. After remembering that her mother had been "really mad" and had said something about cutting her hair off, she recalled her mother's favorite angry expression: "I'm going to wring your neck."

Nancy began a subsequent session by describing how vulnerable she'd been feeling. She'd been thinking about yearning for love from her parents, and was "hurting a lot." Hearing a feeling word, I slowed my words and asked her the following question: "And as you're hurting a lot, where are you hurting a lot as you're hurting a lot?" Nancy clearly located the feeling in her chest. It was above her heart, "but not deep, something that's exposed, other people can see it . . . Mom will hurt it." As I was not sure whether Nancy was accessing a memory, I asked, "Is there anything else?" Nancy replied, "want to tell Mom I love her . . . I'm afraid." Sensing that Nancy was talking about an earlier experience, I asked her how old "afraid" was. She responded, "seven," and began sharing some new memories with me.

Nancy talked about a teacher, "Miss Abbott," who wore "pink . . . sang . . . and smelled good. . . . Her hands were very soft." The profusion of sensory information about Miss Abbott led me to believe that this teacher was very important to Nancy. My suspicion was confirmed, for Nancy said that she had wanted this teacher to worry about her. But then Miss Abbott chose someone else to demonstrate something to the class and Nancy realized that she couldn't have been that special to her.

The memory of Miss Abbott led to recollections of other painful incidents involving the death of a favorite kitten and some additional interactions with her mother. By the end of the session Nancy had recalled a series of devastating experiences entailing the loss of someone or something she loved. Although I do not know whether we can go so far as to stay that these memories were stored in Nancy's chest, they did enter consciousness when she attended to the area where "hurting a lot" was located. Nancy described this process as one in which the "images come at me so fast . . . powerful feeling . . . overcome by emotions and images."

Although Nancy had never allowed herself to admit that her mother was abusive, she came to this conclusion without my ever using the word *abuse*. This previously disowned information shed new light on how her relationship with her mother had influenced the way she related to her husband. By engaging with dispossessed parts of herself, Nancy felt herself becoming "freer to be myself."

Nancy readily tapped into the underlying issues that were contributing to the problems she was having with her husband. Some clients, however, have more difficulty with this process. These people appear to be more disconnected from aspects of their experiences, more dissociated from parts of their selves. Their wounds are deeper, the scars more hidden. Re-membering could be re-traumatizing.

It is important to avoid re-traumatizing clients. They don't need to relive traumatic experiences in order to re-member their-selves. Working with metaphors and other symbols is a way of helping clients relate to the dissociated parts of themselves. I've been taking this approach with Sarah.

Sarah came to therapy with a myriad of presenting problems. She had difficulty relating to others and felt "sensitive . . . odd . . . lonely . . . sad . . . always scared." During our first session I asked many questions about her past. Although I don't routinely inquire about abuse, something she said must have clued me into the possibility, for I asked whether she had been abused. She recalled a time when her brother had blackmailed her into letting him perform cunnilingus. In addition, she related an occasion during late adolescence when her father had made a sexual advance but then stopped. These were the only memories she had of sexual abuse.

As our work progressed I gradually began suspecting that there were other occasions when Sarah had been abused. She had major memory gaps and reported dissociated experiences – times when she felt separate from her body. In addition, she told me about occasions when she was compelled to go into her bathroom, sit on the floor, rock, make noises, hold herself, and sometimes mutilate herself.

While I don't have the space here to share all that emerged during the course of Sarah's lengthy therapy, I do want to mention that I worked with her in many different ways. At times I explained what I thought was happening. I shared my suspicions with her, told her how I arrived at certain conclusions. When she didn't trust her own experiences and worried that she might be lying, I explained what we know about people who have been abused and encouraged her to start trusting her own perceptions.

Sarah complained about not knowing how to talk about what was troubling her. She kept saying that as she didn't have words, she would need to show me, act something out with me. She also told me that I would need to do something to her, force something out of her.

Although I discouraged Sarah from acting out her feelings in self-destructive ways, I did encourage her to use symbolic avenues of expression. She used a range of creative vehicles to express what she was feeling inside. For example, she made a type of sculpture using a clip and some wire to describe the feeling of a clip that was being held wide open but was trying to close. At other times she made pictures of what she had talked about during a session.

While I generally refrained from making interpretations of Sarah's drawings, on one occasion her comments led me to believe that she had seen what I had seen, a phallic shape. I made a brief comment about this shape, but she didn't pick up on it until the next session when she said, "Those pictures didn't come from my head. . . . My head won't own the pictures 'cause it doesn't know that. . . . My head thinks I'm lying. . . . It's only OK for my hand to draw if it doesn't know what it's doing." During the next session Sarah said, "Nothing is wrong with my head . . . what's wrong with me is in my body . . . I want to work with my body."

Sarah had trouble identifying where her feelings were located. She knew she had a body, but said she never went there. She lived in her head. As Sarah's body and mind were split, I looked for ways in which her body could begin to be heard.

During one particular session Sarah admitted feeling angry toward me. Although she was uncomfortable with this feeling, she talked about it anyway. After discussing a number of related issues she said, "I just had the strangest sensation to bite you."

We didn't have time to explore Sarah's strange sensation until the following session. Sarah went back to it then, this time describing it as a "little urge." Because Sarah lived in her head, I had learned not to ask where her feelings were located. Instead, I asked about the bite, about what kind of bite it might be. She said, "If I was going to bite you, I would bite you on the shoulder." I modulated my voice and continued inquiring about the bite, repeating her statement that she would bite me on the shoulder, and asking whether there was anything else.

Sarah answered, "I would bite hard . . . one time. . . . I know it hurt." Noting that she had switched to the past tense, I too changed tenses and continued my inquiry by again repeating her words and asking if there was anything else. She said, "It didn't hurt me 'cause I was all teeth at the time. . . . I wanted it to hurt. . . . I see ugly gross teeth and I'm kind of watching it . . . I don't remember letting go. . . . It was me and that skin. . . . Remember scared and sad, not angry."

The above material was one of many interactions I had with Sarah in which she appeared to access a memory fragment. A sensation in the here and now had contained a message from her past. As our therapy progressed, Sarah began communicating with her body and became able to identify where her feelings were located. She also started complaining of pains in her neck, back, and shoulders. These pains had probably been with her all along, even though she had not felt them.

While many of these examples have involved accessing memories, I am not suggesting that psychotherapy is a memory-retrieval process. Clients may be able to connect with repressed, suppressed, and otherwise dissociated aspects of themselves without recalling the original incidents that led to dis-memberment. And although Nancy's re-membering process was very different from Sarah's, they were both able to assimilate previously disowned parts of their selves.

Recollection isn't re-membering. Re-membering invites crossing over – a coming together with previously dispossessed aspects of the self. Lost voices are given opportunities to be heard and therefore no longer need to use symptoms as their mouthpieces. Clients resume growing by integrating their selves into a whole way of being.

Hearing

Good therapists are good listeners. We use all of our senses, our many kinds of ears, in hearing what clients are trying to say. And while most clients look to us to lead, we must take direction from them by listening to their messages, hearing where they need to go, and endeavoring to help them move in that direction.

Psychotherapy involves using all of our inner resources in attending to clients. As our thoughts, feelings, and associations can contribute to a session, we listen at every level of our being. We listen between the lines of conversation, hearing not only words, but also their underlying meanings.

The psychotherapist's way of hearing is sensitive to interference. Our inner messages often contain clues to clients' internal processes, but they lead us astray when they are tainted by our own needs, interests, feelings, and past history. By sifting through our responses, we learn to sense if our own issues are intruding into a therapy session. Countertransference is useful for what it tells us about a client, but unconscious projections from our own inner lives onto clients aren't useful to them and can be detrimental to therapy. Such interference needs to be recognized, understood, and weeded out.

Although I am generally attuned to clients, there are times when my hearing is impaired. One such occasion occurred when a client, Nina, began talking about wanting to go on vacation. She was feeling ambivalent and confused about what to do.

As Nina had been in therapy with me for quite some time, I was accustomed to addressing her underlying issues and opted to continue doing so in this session. Instead of discussing how Nina might proceed with making vacation plans, where she might wish to go and when, I focused on her confusion. After asking where her confusion was located and what it was like when it was there, I persisted with this line of inquiry. When Nina started telling me she was feeling frustrated, I asked her where "frustrated" was located, etc. At the end of the session Nina looked me straight in the eye and let me know that she had wanted to make a decision about where to go on her vacation. It had not been the time to explore inner confusion.

Nina had wanted to make plans for the future. Since I was more interested in her confusion, I committed the cardinal sin of allowing my interest to determine the direction of *her* therapy. She taught me a lesson that every therapist re-learns from time to time. We need to own our mistakes and I usually admit mine to clients. While I don't share personal reasons for lapses in hearing, I will acknowledge them. Regardless of how we may deal with these types of mistakes, each blunder is a sign that our hearing was impaired – a reminder to turn up our hearing aids and listen even more carefully to what clients are trying to say.

Client issues are frequently not far removed from our own. As human beings, we often share similar experiences. These similarities can be helpful. Our hard-earned insights into our own human dilemmas serve as bridges that help us hear clients and point them toward their own inner discoveries.

Most therapists listen with inner as well as outer ears. We switch back and forth, tuning in to different channels, listening to clients' words, seeing their facial expressions, noting other sensory cues, and hearing our own inner messages. Sometimes we respond with a feeling, sometimes an idea. Before translating these responses into words, we check to make sure that they're not contaminated by our own issues.

When a female client, Donna, recently came in for her first therapy session, I had already formed a tentative impression from our telephone conversation. She had mentioned that she was seeking therapy because she felt weighed down, burdened, depressed. I was reminded of the many women I see with similar complaints. Some of these women are overweight, others are not. However, they have usually tuned out their own inner voice while channeling most of their energies outside of themselves, taking care of other people.

Women's issues are one of my specialties. In addition to reading extensively in the field, I have personally grappled with these issues and have written a book on the subject (Shore, 1992d). I believe that while everyone suffers the consequences of society's worship of the masculine and repression of the feminine, females are placed in a particularly difficult position because they are also expected to express the feminine.

If a female identifies with the feminine, she then admits into her sense of herself that which is devalued by society. This is a double bind, a no-win situation, for then there is something inherently wrong with her. This psychological dilemma has far-reaching consequences for females who inadvertently collude with society's war against the feminine by battling this central aspect of their selves. In my opinion, this dilemma is often the underlying dynamic behind a woman's tendency to develop eating disorders, dissociate, feel ashamed, and try to please. And while this knowledge of women would probably prove useful in my work with Donna, I knew that I would need to guard against projecting my theories and feelings onto her.

After entering the office and completing the usual forms and introductions, we began discussing Donna's difficulty. She described an inexplicable "heavy weight" in her chest. It "weighs" her "down" all the time, making every aspect of her life feel like a major effort, "Everything's a burden, a chore."

When I asked Donna to further elucidate this sensation, she described feeling as if everything is on her shoulders, "weighing" her "down," making it hard to get out of bed in the morning. Once out of bed, she barely has energy to care for children she dearly loves. It's difficult to move, let alone clean house, make dinner, or bake cookies for the church fair.

Listening to Donna, I heard her metaphors screaming for attention and felt tempted to explore the meanings ascribed to her "weight." However, this type of inquiry is premature for a first session. Even if it might help explain why she felt so "down," the metaphors would need to wait until we had settled the question of whether we would be working together.

Continuing to describe her troubles, Donna complained about becoming a burden to her husband. Her frequent crying concerns and worries him. Although he offers suggestions and tries to be helpful, she is afraid he's becoming impatient and fed up with her.

Looking at me with tears in her eyes, Donna desperately pleaded for my help, asking, "What can I do, how can I get rid of this feeling?"

The question was barely out of Donna's mouth before she began chiding herself for having these feelings, and berating herself for not fully appreciating all that she has in life. "Others are worse off than I" she informed me, recognizing that her husband never beat her and that she wasn't starving. She recited all the benefits that life had bestowed on her: she lives in a beautiful home, her husband has a good job, and she has three healthy, thriving children. Again looking in my direction, Donna asked "Why can't I appreciate all that I have, and just be happy?" Despite all of her purported external abundance, she is haunted by "this weight," "this heaviness."

As Donna continued her litany of self-deprecation, she accused herself of being "ungrateful" and feeling sorry for herself. She was ashamed to be in my office, crying, when others were not as fortunate as she. Reminders of her plentiful life were supposed to make her feel better.

As I listened to Donna struggle, I heard her looking to me for answers to unformed questions. Instead of listening to herself, she was battling with her self, trying to control "it." And so I began the process of directing Donna's attention toward her self, inviting her to hear her inner voice and trust that her perceptions and feelings were real. I voiced my observation that she didn't appear to feel entitled to feelings that obviously troubled her, indirectly suggesting that Donna value herself by listening to these feelings and granting them credibility.

Our session continued. Donna had begun sharing her litany of distress, but I had to give witness, provide verbal feedback for all that was troubling her before she could start hearing herself. With tears spilling down her cheeks, she confessed that she has difficulty with her "weight." While she knows what she should do to lose weight, she has been unable to motivate herself in this direction. Donna's inability to lose weight was presented as the ultimate proof of her failure in life.

Hearing Donna's cry for help, I asked her to describe this difficulty with her "weight." She spoke of being driven to eat, though she's not certain of whether she feels hungry at the time. During moments of being alone, having driven her children to a piano lesson or watched them go out to play, she eats unconsciously – driven by an out-of-awareness hunger, a hunger she can neither name nor describe. It's as if there's an internal void that never gets filled. As I listened to Donna's words, I was reminded of other clients with similar stories.

After finishing the first stanza, Donna moved on to the next familiar refrain. Whenever she overeats she feels ashamed and resolves to diet the very next day. These resolutions readily evaporate into thin air, for she is again driven to "overeat." As Donna didn't volunteer the information, I gently asked about her eating patterns, knowing that there is always more to tell.

Like most women in this society, I too have struggled with my "weight." As I have also eaten compulsively, I had a feeling for what Donna was talking about. I am, in various ways, knowledgeable about eating disorders. But while I knew that this knowledge might eventually prove useful to Donna, I first needed to hear her story. More importantly, she needed to tell her story and have someone hear it.

Although relieved to be finally sharing her secrets, Donna was mortified to admit that she consumes most of the cookies and candy she buys for the children; she then runs to the store to replenish "their" supplies. Donna pretends she is buying "junk food" for them, only to yield to the temptation to consume the latest batch before her children arrive home from school. Again Donna berated herself, "It's so embarrassing to be unable to control these urges. If only I could begin to control myself I would feel so much better."

Listening to all this, I recalled Donna's earlier refrain of another weighty matter – the one in her chest and the ones on her shoulders that were "weighing" her "down." As I continued inquiring into various aspects of her life, Donna began unburdening her soul, speaking about the load she bears – the burden of caring about other people's feelings, the burden of being everyone's caretaker, the burden of carrying the world "on her shoulders." She also spoke of pressures in relationships, for everyone expects her to give. She gives and gives, but feels empty, depleted, given out.

It was time to end our session. After scheduling our next appointment, Donna spoke of having "gotten a load off" her chest, of feeling "lighter." She had looked inward, shared her burden, and lightened her load.

I watched Donna leaving my office. Her made-up face was streaked with blotches of mascara, reminders of tears that had escaped her sad eyes. She tottered out of the office, perched atop high heels that were obviously uncomfortable, wearing shoes that appeared far too small for her feet. Her feet cried out to me of their burdens and I recalled the saying: If the shoe fits, wear it. I wondered how long it would take before Donna noticed that her shoes don't fit, and whether she would be able to find ones that do.

Later I changed my shoes, preparing for a walk. I continued musing about women and shoes. Women are known for being able to put themselves in other people's shoes, for being empathetic, for understanding another person's position, situation, or feeling. We readily take on other people's burdens, make them our own, and become caretakers, pleasers who wear uncomfortable shoes to suit a conventional eye. Perhaps we do this too readily, without first rooting in shoes of our own.

After settling into walking shoes, I noticed that my feet felt heavier than usual. Therapists readily become weighed down, burdened, for we absorb client issues into ourselves. While these concerns usually leave when the client walks out the door, sometimes they remain with us. As issues from a session may continue reverberating inside us, we must learn ways of letting go of them and moving on with our own lives.

Like other therapists, I usually leave ten minutes between appointments to shift from one client to another. This gives me time to reflect on the session and say goodbye to any residual concerns. But sometimes an issue returns to haunt me at the end of the day. It begins calling to me, demanding my attention.

Listening to my concerns and hearing what they have to say usually teaches me something important about myself as well as my clients. While I've found that taking a walk helps me hear the voices reverberating inside, other therapists might prefer another way of listening. It doesn't matter how we listen, as long as we do.

Reminding myself that walking helps lighten my load, I opened the door, stepped outside, and took a breath of fresh air. The crisp, clear, cool air tingled in my nostrils and cleared cobwebs from my brain. I took a moment to marvel at the scenery, for the sun was casting its late afternoon glow over the landscape. The colors were shining – glistening, twinkling, and sparkling. After a few more deep breaths and some stretches, I was ready to walk.

As my feet touched the ground, sensing life in the earth, they began keeping time with an inner rhythm, harmonizing with nature. My arms began swinging, joining the rhythm, moving back and forth along with my feet. Eventually my whole body merged with the rhythm. I became the rhythm. And as my feet and heart beat their drums together, I was transported into another dimension, another time zone.

Time stood still and I entered the stillness, disappearing inside myself, travelling down internal rivers, flowing, enjoying my inner garden. I began hearing a female voice, an earthy musical voice. Her soft gentle tones joined my feet and kept time with their rhythm. And as I listened to that voice, I heard her telling me that women need to take off their shoes, put their feet on the ground, touch the soil of the earth and connect with the feminine, the Grandmother. A woman needs to send her roots down there, become firmly rooted in the soil of her female self.

Later, having finished my walk, I noticed that I too felt lighter. My feet had touched the earth. My journey within had replenished the soil of my self. I heard what I needed to hear.

Openness

I recently attended a Harvard Medical School conference on psychological trauma. A good friend and colleague, Dr. Priscilla Cogan, accompanied me. We absorbed presentations from scientists about research into the biochemical aspects of trauma. I learned of physiological reasons for the numbing, hyperreactivity, flashbacks and somatic reactions experienced by traumatized individuals: Changes occur in the central nervous system's catecholamine, serotonin, and endogenous opioid systems (Van Der Kolk & Saporta, 1991).

The conference organizers recognized that while biochemical research might be very interesting, its implications for therapy were also important. Bessel Van Der Kolk discussed the usefulness of systematic desensitization as well as medications like Prozac. Judith Herman described her three-stage model for working with traumatized women, which involves developing safety for the victim, exploring the traumatic experience in-depth, and social reconnecting. We attended many other presentations during two intense days of sitting with over 200 other interested individuals in the cramped quarters of an erratically air-conditioned hotel meeting room.

Despite our discomfort, Priscilla and I tried to keep our minds open, waiting for any new information that might be helpful in our work. As we are both seasoned therapists, much of what we heard wasn't new. But the biochemical research interested us both. It shed new light on our work, highlighting the importance of safety.

Priscilla was staying with us on Harmony Farm, so we spent quite a bit of time together, travelling in and out of Boston, taking walks, eating meals, and enjoying each other's company. We shared intimacies about our lives, spoke of our writing, and discussed cases. Our ramblings covered ideas about multiple selves (another conceptualization uses the term *ego states*).

My first exposure to the concept of multiple ego states came through psychosynthesis, a general genre of techniques purported to promote an individual's growth by facilitating communication with his or her various subpersonalities (see *Synthesis*, 1974, 1975, 1977). Psychosynthesis techniques haven't gained much favor over the years, but clinical experience with multiple personalities has revived interest in the notion that people posses multiple selves (Roberts, 1992). According to these ideas, multiplicity is normal, but difficulties arise when these different selves are not integrated into a balanced whole. This lack of integration arises when one or more ego states dominate the system, or if different states are blocked off from one another and are, therefore, unable to communicate with each other.

During our discussion, Priscilla happened to mention Watkins and Watkins ego-state therapy, for she had used this approach with one of her clients (Watkins & Watkins, 1991; Watkins, 1992). At my request, Priscilla described one technique in more detail. It involves four basic phases. In the first, a particular problem or issue is explored in all its dimensions, recognizing that dissimilar internal viewpoints represent different ego states. Once this is done, the characteristics of each ego state are further defined and delineated by giving them names, ages, and other identifying characteristics. Steps three and four entail encouraging communication between the different ego states and having them find new ways of working together.

The conference ended, Priscilla left, and I returned to my practice feeling enriched by all that had happened. Quite honestly, I can't define what I actually took from that conference into my office. I didn't directly transplant something that was said into any one particular therapy session. And I have no idea how my body-mind system processed all the information, integrating it with all that I already knew. But I do know that because I was open, I assimilated the material and it influenced my work.

As I had expressed interest in ego-state therapy, Priscilla sent me a one-page summary of the "chair technique" (Watkins, H. H.). A couple of weeks later, I began wondering whether one particular client, Marie, might find it a helpful way of exploring her eating disorder. Although Marie claimed to have made many gains during four months of therapy, she felt frustrated that her compulsive eating hadn't abated. Acting on an intuitive impulse, I described the chair technique and asked if she might be interested in trying it sometime. Marie eagerly jumped on the idea, asking that we start during the following session. Even though Watkins generally recommends an initial two-hour session, I agreed to try it with Marie at our next scheduled meeting.

During the week, I reviewed the material Priscilla had sent. When Marie arrived at her appointed time, she repeated her interest in ego-state therapy. The chair technique usually involves placing chairs in a circle around the room, but as my office isn't that large, I used pillows instead. Marie sat on each pillow, one by one, speaking about different aspects of her eating. I recorded what she said, suggesting she move to the next pillow each time I heard a different feeling or attitude expressed. Then I placed my notes on the vacated pillow.

Marie started by talking about a feeling of uncertainty, of not being sure she could isolate different voices. Recognizing this as her first ego state, I transcribed her words and waited for a shift. Immediately afterward, Marie mentioned feeling overwhelmed, let down, and disappointed that her eating hadn't changed. I suggested she move to the next pillow; now we had two ego states. We continued with this process until Marie exhausted all the feelings connected with her eating. By this time we had 12 pillows around the room.

Although we were approaching the end of our time, Marie elected to move on to the next phase. I took my notes from the first pillow, suggested she take that seat, read her previous statement back, and encouraged her to describe this voice more fully. I used the word *voice*, because that had been her word, a word she initially adopted from my book (Shore, 1992d) and had used during previous sessions.

Marie identified the voice as "my drowning voice," and decided to call it by that name. When I asked "How old is my drowning voice?" She answered, "eight years old." I waited a while, seeing if she would add anything else, for I recalled that she had once told me about an experience of having almost drowned. Although I had no idea whether ego-state therapy usually includes such questions, I recalled the drowning experience for Marie and asked how old she had been. Marie glanced at me with a look of amazement, said "eight," then smiled. Having made a connection, she moved on to the next pillow.

Again I read my notes, recalling Marie's description of feeling overwhelmed, sinking, and disappointed. She labelled this voice "my depression," and talked about feeling like a lost child. As we had run out of time, we stopped at this point. I gathered up my notes, keeping the ego states in order so that we could resume where we left off.

When Marie came in for her next appointment, she spoke about how useful the previous session had been, but then mentioned a crisis that needed our attention. While this was not the time to continue the procedure, we incorporated her experience with ego-state therapy into our discussion of the crisis. Soon after, she left for vacation, indicating that when she returned she wanted to continue the ego-state therapy. She claimed to have already gained from the exercise.

I wish I could describe what happened with Marie's ego-state therapy, because I had planned to try hypnotic techniques (Edelstein, 1981; Watkins, 1992), and was curious about what might happen. But a therapist must always be open, ready to respond to unexpected turns of events. If we become too invested in one particular technique or line of inquiry, we close ourselves off from important possibilities. As I was open to the idea of trying ego-state therapy, I discovered an approach that could prove useful with clients. Moreover, I enjoyed throwing myself into another role. The chair technique not only brought out Marie's ego states but accessed another of my own – the playful child.

With the gardener supervising, the playful child had joined the scientist and wise woman. These various parts of my self, and probably some others, helped guide Marie's exploration. They each played their role in the session. The gardener remained open, listening to the voices, directing the work and its play.

The gardener is my main therapist personality. The gardener oversees everything I do, deciding what should happen when. During most therapy sessions the wise woman offers her love and caring, her intuition, and her good common sense. The scientist provides his order, his distance, his logic and reason. But the playful potential of ego-state therapy also called for a child.

Many therapeutic tools call for the child within us. Interpreting dreams, looking at drawings, using humor – all require a sense of play. The child also offers curiosity, an essential ingredient of therapy. My child also likes mysteries. And movies.

Although I go to movies for pleasure, good movies reverberate through every part of my life, including my work. Sometimes a character reminds me of a client. This isn't surprising because movies, like books, are basically about people and their life issues. And while I learn from the stories, like with the conference, the lesson can't be directly transferred into a particular therapy session. I can, however, recommend the lesson itself.

As there are many ways of promoting growth, I frequently recommend specific movies and books. This year, for example, has seen some good movies about women. I particularly enjoyed *Strangers in Good Company*, a Canadian film that manages to communicate the beauty inside every woman. It dealt more with older women, a group particularly maligned in our current world, and celebrated the feminine value of caring and connection while showing unique individual selves (Shore, 1992a). I recommended it to clients whom I felt would benefit from hearing its message. The movie touched them deeply.

Books also convey important messages. I like suggesting novels to clients, for stories are teaching tales. It's important, however, not to make recommendations haphazardly. In order for a story to be helpful, it must tap into a client's particular issues.

Many clients are eager to work on their problems and want suggestions about books that directly address their difficulties. In my experience, many women benefit from reading a book like *The Dance of Anger* by Harriet Goldhor Lerner. Books like *Fat Is a Feminist Issue* by Susie Orbach, *Overcoming Overeating* by Jane Hirschmann and Carol Munter, and *Breaking Free from Compulsive Eating* by Geneen Roth can be helpful for eating-disordered clients. And as I believe that women need to accept their bodies, not fight their fat, I like recommending a *Woman of Power* issue called "Women's Bodies" (Issue 18, Fall 1990). But again, every recommendation must be tailor-made.

How do I arrive at such suggestions? The only way to answer that question is with the word openness. My gardener stays open, tending the whole garden, soliciting advice from the wise woman

and heeding the scientist's skeptical judgment. The scientist tests
the soil. The wise woman looks at it, feels it, smells it, and tastes it.
And my child runs around, playing with ways that might reach into
a client's imagination. I remain open to everyone, listening to what
they have to say. Then, trusting the guidance of the gardener, I
decide what to do.

Guidance comes from many sources. Having been a therapist for
such a long time, much of that guidance is now internal. But it's
also important to consult with other people.

Psychotherapy is a complex process, fraught with threats of sui-
cide, impending divorce, and other critical, potentially catastrophic,
dilemmas. It is also a private affair, guarded by rules of confidentiality that preclude chatting with a spouse or a friend, sharing
details of one's day. But therapists are only human. We all make
mistakes, especially when we don't step back and view our work
from another perspective. It is, therefore, important that each therapist have opportunities to consult with other people and learn from
their views.

During my early years as a therapist, I was regularly supervised
by professionals more experienced than myself. After becoming a
supervisor, I regularly consulted with someone else in the organiza-
tion. When I moved into private practice, these arrangements were
no longer available, yet I wanted to continue receiving input from
others. I was faced with the choice of either arranging to be supervised by another professional or establishing my own peer supervision group. As I knew two other women whose work I respected, I
opted for the group.

After working through various complications of time and place,
my peer supervision group gradually became a safe place for exploring our work. Meetings are forums for sharing ideas as well as
feelings. We support each other, grapple with issues together, and
share the joys and sorrows in each of our lives.

Geri, Maida, and I are very different from one another. Our
lifestyles are different. Our styles of therapy are different. What we
do have in common is a commitment to openness – with each other
as well as our selves. Lack of openness promotes strife; but with
openness, diversity enriches. Our differences provide balance, and

our openness enables us to learn from each other and to grow together.

People generally think of openness as a state of mind. And perhaps there is no specific location, only space. Openness is space for finding balance, making connections, and synthesizing every facet of the self. It is space for hearing voices – of the gardener, the wise woman, the scientist, the child, and a detective who enjoys piecing together clues to human mysteries. Cultivating openness is the key to tending inner gardens – our own as well as our clients.

Seasons

Process

Psychotherapy is a creative process. It is a growth process for ourselves as well as our clients. We make new discoveries with each client, in each session, and continue growing as therapists.

Psychotherapy is an art as well as a science. We benefit from knowing as much as we can about research into theories of personality and psychotherapy. But when we sit with a client, we need to trust the art – to have a feel for the person we're with and to trust our sense of where we need to go with that particular person. The art of psychotherapy involves taking all our knowledge and using it to benefit clients. This is, at times, a lonely endeavor, for no two clients are ever the same, and no two sessions can ever be repeated. As soon as we figure out how to help one person in one session, we are faced with the next session, another person, another difficulty, another therapy.

Each therapy is a journey into new terrain. To create guidelines for this journey – a road map for ourselves or to share with colleagues – we look for principles, general directions to follow. Although therapy refuses to follow a set series of events, a pattern usually develops over time. It isn't a fixed schema, but a sequence of recurring happenings – a process inherent in the nature of psychotherapy.

As therapy moves from one phase to another it follows a fundamental sequence frequently found in nature. This sequence is the cycle of creativity – an organic process – the natural progression of events by which old patterns are converted into new relationships.

The yearly movement from fall through winter, into spring and then summer is nature's rebirthing process – her creative dance. As this cycle is similar to the process I keep observing in my office, it has become my way of charting psychotherapy, keeping track of its progress. Nature's seasonal cycle is a model for psychotherapy.

While psychotherapy seems to proceed in a seasonal manner, this sequence isn't a linear progression. Each phase does lead to the next, but seasons don't follow a straight route. Seasons flow in, out, and around each other. They act like the tide moving in – rippling back and forth and back and forth, gradually edging in on the shore. Sometimes a season may appear to move more directly, like the tidal bore in Nova Scotia where water courses along a narrow path. But, even then, there is a subtle eddying to the seasonal cycle, such as when welcòme waves of spring temper long cold winters.

Therapy sessions follow a similar pattern, for they never travel in straight lines. One topic flows into another, then pulls back, picking up another wave. And while one process is taking place on the surface, something else can be occurring below.

In proposing that psychotherapy moves through seasons, I'm not suggesting a particular time frame for therapy. Psychotherapy aims to shift, to change, and the length of therapy is determined by how long it takes clients to accomplish their goals. Psychotherapy isn't necessarily a long-term process, but there are usually no instant solutions to long-standing difficulties. Symptoms generally need to be addressed from many angles before their underlying processes will shift. Change takes time.

Psychotherapy travels through a more dormant period of winter to the active growth of spring, but not everyone goes through each phase in the same way. Each personality has its own growing conditions. These individual growth cycles are comparable to living in different regions of the country: Each area has its own way of moving through seasons. But even though one area's winter is colder than another's, nature's growing cycle follows a seasonal pattern.

While the process of therapy takes place over time, another important dimension is that of space. Therapists take both dimensions into account when responding to clients. We time our interventions by sensing each garden's growing condition.

By attending to clients, we continually assess the condition of their soil. Every garden has a history that is uniquely its own. Whatever has happened to it in the past determines its present growing condition – whether soil is depleted or rich in minerals and full of organic matter, whether the land is fertile or barren, and whether it is hard and compacted or loose and friable.

Gardeners assess the soil's current condition before deciding which tools to use in the garden, and psychotherapists similarly adjust their styles to suit each client's particular situation. For example, gardeners refrain from digging in wet soil because this procedure tends to compact the earth. Under certain circumstances, psychological digging will also produce a form of compaction called resistance.

There are many parallels between the earth in the garden and the soil inside ourselves. Therapists are gardeners. Using whatever tools are available to us and continually modifying our tools to suit the occasion, we do whatever we can to promote growth. While one therapy calls for certain tools more than others, another therapy may require a totally different set of tools. We also adapt each of our tools for every session. No two therapies ever use the same tools in an identical way.

Experienced psychotherapists learn to trust their art. In addition to using many tools, we vary our tools according to the season. What works in one season may not work in another. Becoming aware of the seasons keeps us in tune with the process.

The following chapters will describe the process of psychotherapy through its seasons of fall, winter, spring, and summer. I have chosen to follow one person through the seasons of her therapy in order to provide a sense of continuity. In doing so, however, I do not intend to suggest that everyone goes through exactly the same process in the same way. The art of psychotherapy is its creative process.

Fall

Fall is a busy time in the garden. The sun continues to shine, but its angle is changing; it's dropping closer to the horizon, moving farther and farther away. As the air and soil gradually cool, we're reminded that winter is around the corner. Gardeners prepare growing areas for the seasons ahead. We focus our attention on the soil – protecting it from the ravages of winter while also making sure it's ready for the spurt of growth that comes with spring. These preparations include tilling in the remnants of this year's garden, adding compost, raking, and mulching. We say goodbye to the old and provide the groundwork for the new.

Therapy often begins in fall. After summer winds down and children go off to school, my phone starts ringing. Having observed this phenomenon over and over again, I've come to expect it as a sign of fall. Like plants pulling energy back into their roots, people similarly move inside their homes and retreat into themselves. It's nature's time for starting an inner journey.

Therapy provides a context, a format for the inner journey. People begin turning in toward themselves, listening to their feelings, motivations, desires, and internal yearnings. While therapy is not necessary for this journey to occur, it is a way of marking it – establishing an intention to begin paying attention to inside, focusing on what's there, and having something happen there. It's like marking the site for a future garden. The plan is laid out, a place established, an intention formed.

Therapists, like gardeners, need to keep an eye on the seasons. Fall is the season for laying the beds, preparing soil for future growth. This includes structuring the therapeutic relationship, cultivating a connection, establishing the groundwork for what we will be doing together.

Many of my colleagues view the therapeutic relationship as one of a doctor with a patient. These colleagues have generally worked in hospitals and clinics, settings that tend to follow the medical model. Other colleagues use a consultant model that is more prevalent in business and educational settings. They view the therapeutic relationship as one of a professional with a client. Having worked in both types of settings and abided by their models, I prefer living with an organic gardening model – a model that is rooted in nature.

I look to establish open, honest, respectful, and supportive relationships with the people who come to see me, and see the work we do as a collaborative effort. While I've been referring to these people as *clients*, I'm not happy with this term because, like the word *patient*, it implies a hierarchical structure. Our current vocabulary doesn't have words for the kind of relationship I aim to establish with the people who seek my help. Gardeners work *with* natural processes; we don't have power over them.

As I want to let people know that my credentials include a doctoral diploma, I usually introduce myself as Dr. Lesley Shore. But since I want clients to feel free to call me Lesley, I add a statement to that effect, inviting them to call me by whatever name feels comfortable for them. While most clients call me Lesley, some prefer to use the term Doctor. Often these people eventually develop their own way of referring to me. One adolescent girl seemed to enjoy greeting me with an affectionate "Hiya Doc!"

Susan called me Lesley.

I will be talking about Susan's therapy throughout this section. She was referred to me by her minister who recognized that she would benefit from psychotherapy. I saw her for a period of about four years and will be describing the process of her therapy through its seasons.

People start therapy because they're stuck. They're no longer growing, moving in spirals, but going round and around, trapped in self-perpetuating cycles. Usually they've tried to shift the cycle on their own but have been unable to resolve their difficulties. The same pattern, or symptom, keeps repeating itself, and they turn to a professional for help.

The initial session is extremely important because it sets the stage for therapy. It lays the foundation for the road ahead, and many things happen at this time. While we need to deal with practical matters (business details such as fees and insurance information) our primary concern is the client's emotional state.

Most people begin therapy hoping for an immediate solution to problems that have been troubling them for many years. They're looking for prescriptions and are ready to swallow advice. But psychotherapy is a process. It's necessary to explore the roots of a symptom, the seed of the difficulty, and we usually have no quick fixes to offer clients. Deep-seated problems can't generally be resolved in one or two sessions.

Instead of offering pills, we offer ourselves. Because we're familiar with the growing process, we know ways of helping people shift from stuck positions. We can help them grow.

People seek our assistance when they're in crisis. They're compelled by emotional distress, and we must address their despair. They need to feel that someone will help them, that something can happen, something can shift. The relationship we establish with clients is, therefore, of the utmost importance. If we're honest and open with them, sharing our knowledge and responding to their questions, they can begin to hope. And hope is the first step toward healing.

When I first met Susan I was struck by her lack of hope. She seemed worn out, drained, and I had the distinct impression that she had stopped caring about herself. While her clothing was presentable and neat, its drab colors matched her lifeless facial expression. Her body posture communicated the same information, for her shoulders drooped and her head hung heavy. She seemed to be sinking into the ground.

Susan began telling me about herself and I wasn't surprised to hear that she was depressed. In her words, "I'm sad, just sad." Having lived in the area for only three years, she still felt as if she had no friends. And while the last three years had been the most stable of her life, she kept expecting something bad to happen, waiting for the axe to fall, and kept wanting to scream and cry.

Knowing that her current situation was one facet of a larger picture, I inquired about other aspects of her life. Susan readily spoke about her past, telling me about the tragedy of losing her first husband shortly after having given birth to their first child. She later married another man, and they adopted three more children. In addition to these four children, she was also stepmother to another four children from her husband's previous marriage.

Moving further back in time, Susan described herself as having been a "pushed kid." She was the oldest child and had been given a great deal of responsibility in the family. Her father suffered from a severe ulcer condition and was often ill and always irritable. While she and her sister kept their mouths shut, her two brothers fought with their father.

Susan had done well in school. She had graduated from a good college and had previously been employed, but was no longer working because of her duties in the home. Describing herself as "super-responsible," she added "I'm tired of this, but can't quit."

After addressing her general situation, Susan went on to tell me about her weight problem. She'd been struggling with her weight for quite some time and had previously managed to lose a few pounds. However, she hadn't felt motivated to do anything about her weight because the only one it hurt was herself. And while she knew about the importance of exercise, she didn't feel entitled to take the time that walking required.

The only bright spot in her life appeared to be the piano. She had recently resumed taking piano lessons, but was having difficulty finding time to practice. Even though she enjoyed playing the piano, like with walking, she couldn't justify taking the time to do it.

Listening to Susan describe herself, I recognized that she was no longer growing in the spiral of a natural cycle. Natural cycles may have a repetitive quality, but they move on in time and on in space, on to the next phase, the next cycle. As natural cycles are open systems, ever ready to react to new influences and unexpected turns of events, they never stay stuck in the same place. Susan's cycle wasn't moving, shifting, and changing. She was definitely stuck.

As our session neared a close, I began summarizing our discussion. I let her know that with four children in the home (eight in all), it was no wonder she was feeling tired, depleted, worn out. However, this inherently complicated situation was being compounded by her tendency to devote herself to others while neglecting herself. As this unbalanced pattern of constantly trying to please people seemed to date back to her early years, working through the roots of this difficulty might help resume her growing process. And while I couldn't make any promises about what would happen, I offered to support her efforts to develop the stunted parts of herself.

After Susan indicated that she would like to make another appointment, I handed her a few pages of information that I give to all my new clients. One section details my fees and policies regarding cancellations, no-shows, and other billing issues. The other section is a statement regarding the legal limits of therapeutic confidentiality. I encouraged Susan to read this material and bring in any questions she may have about it.

During our next session Susan struggled with the question of whether to continue therapy. Even though she and her family could afford the expense, she didn't feel entitled to spend money on herself. After recognizing that the financial issue was part of a larger problem – her general lack of entitlement – Susan decided to give therapy a try, and we scheduled a weekly appointment.

Like most therapists, I generally give each client a predictable, consistent time that becomes his or her weekly therapy session. While I usually see clients once a week, I recommend more frequent sessions during times of major crisis. Whenever I recommend more frequent sessions, they too become part of a predictable schedule.

Each psychotherapy session is like adding material to a compost pile. Depending on the circumstances, we sometimes add water; at other times, organic matter. Each session contributes to the composting process. But if we stop adding material, the process may slow down, cool, and even stop. I've found that weekly sessions are necessary in order to keep the process moving and additional sessions can help intensify the experience.

Some clients ask whether they can be seen less frequently than once a week, for they are concerned about the expense of time, money, effort, and energy. And while I'm sympathetic toward the limitations of their resources, I generally recommend that they come once a week. Less frequent sessions don't have the same impact, for compost cools, making it more difficult for clients to effect the hoped-for changes in their lives.

Although we had agreed upon a weekly appointment time, Susan continued struggling with her ambivalence about therapy. She wondered about what she was entitled to want. As the unpleasantries in her family had been kept hidden and she'd been taught not to trust outsiders, she had no guidelines for judging normalcy. She'd been taught that her parents could do no wrong, but sensed that they hadn't been supportive and knew that she had hated being with them. After recognizing that they'd also taught her to feel ashamed, she realized that she wanted to feel better about herself and decided to risk questioning her parents' dictates.

During subsequent sessions, Susan started exploring feelings about her parents, particularly her mother. Her mother was constantly criticizing and accusing, never appreciating what was being done for her. While Susan was angry with her, it took a while before she could use the word *abuse*. After speaking with one of her cousins, she came in for a session saying, "I realize I was abused as a child." She began telling me about her mother slapping her face and her father's violent scenes at the dinner table.

Talking about her mother raised issues about her own mothering. While listening to Susan I heard her own patterns, not those of her mother. She was being overly good, trying to please, doing everything she could for her children. I had the sense that she related to her children like she did to her parents, for she gave them power over her feelings of self-worth – looking to them for approval and feeling uncomfortable when they were critical of her. Unlike her mother, who hadn't cared what Susan felt, Susan was very responsive to her children. I shared these perceptions with Susan, letting her know that I saw her as a good mother, and that being a good mother doesn't preclude feeling angry toward one's children. While it's normal to feel angry, her early years had taught her to be afraid of anger and to identify it with abusive behavior.

When I called Susan a "good mother," tears came to her eyes. She was relieved to hear my comments and understood what I said, but my voice couldn't drown out the years of training. Wishing that people in her life would treat her as she treats them, she kept asking, "What's wrong with me?" "Why aren't I good enough?" And she kept hearing her parents' continual accusations, calling her "ungrateful," "selfish."

From my perspective Susan was far from being selfish or ungrateful. She was inclined to take care of everyone else's needs while disregarding her own. And though I could serve as a voice on Susan's behalf, she needed to hear her own.

I suspected that music might help Susan begin listening to her inner voice; it could provide a pathway into herself. But, as was typical for her, she was busy chauffeuring her children to and from their various activities, and had difficulty finding time for her own. Hearing that she wasn't protecting the time she set aside for practicing the piano and organ, I began encouraging Susan to make time for her music.

As our sessions continued, Susan started listening to her deeper feelings. She felt alone, disconnected, and yearned to feel closer to other people, particularly her husband. And she heard a tiny voice, deep inside. When I inquired more about the voice, she said, "it wants me to have my needs met." The voice was located in the middle of her back and it had walls around it. It was boxed in and confined, but she knew that it wanted recognition, to be of some value to somebody.

In a session shortly after identifying this voice, Susan began talking about her constant inner struggle and turmoil. This tension was located in her stomach. It was associated with waiting – similar to how she felt while waiting to see her exam papers in school. And as she put it in a later session, "There's always this tension inside . . . everything is a struggle, and painful."

Our sessions progressed and Susan's struggle intensified. She felt "alone, separate, apart, not in my body . . . empty." And while she generally didn't know what she wanted, she also couldn't risk asking to have her needs met. Knowing that people have difficulty hearing their own needs while being bombarded by other people's expectations, I encouraged Susan to begin setting aside time to be by herself. She could practice the piano, play the organ, walk, read, or do whatever she wished during this time. I also reiterated the importance of continuing to make time for her music.

Susan had been in therapy for about half a year when she came in saying that she was enjoying her music. While she still complained about having nothing to offer others, she was able to say that music made her happy. This was the first time I had ever heard Susan mention the word *happy* in relation to herself. She went on to say, "I'm happier than I've been in a long time."

While Susan seemed to be feeling slightly better, I knew that she hadn't yet worked through her deeper issues. Her happiness was a good sign, but many clients seem to show some improvement during the early phase of therapy. Usually the improvement comes shortly after starting therapy. Clients show an immediate response to therapy – as if they're basking in the warmth of the therapeutic relationship, which is like a ray of sunshine brightening their lives.

Old patterns are like the leaves of trees. During fall their brilliant colors seem filled with energy and full of life. Holding on to their last breath of life, the leaves put on a magnificent show, displaying glorious hues of reds, oranges, and yellows. The show is usually superficial and short-lived, for inside the sap is withdrawing, closing up. Old patterns can put on a similar show. They fight for survival and clients appear to improve.

When clients start feeling a little better, some are tempted to leave therapy prematurely, before they've addressed their underlying issues. This phase has been called a "flight into health," because the sense of well-being seems to be associated with an unconscious attempt to avoid changing old patterns. Clients appear to be running away from addressing their more problematic, core issues. If this happens, I respect my client's decision to leave therapy, but also share whatever concerns I may have about it.

Our therapy progressed without discussing termination because Susan's fleeting feeling of happiness soon circled back to sadness, frustration, and her continued sense of not being good enough. She talked about feeling constantly under attack, and began identifying that she had trouble with interpersonal conflict, particularly if someone was unhappy with her. And as she couldn't say no to people, she was constantly feeling overwhelmed by the expectations and demands of her family.

Once Susan began connecting with her feelings, she recognized that they were in one place, way deep inside. Her feelings had to be hidden because they weren't acceptable. And while we had primarily been discussing her "hurt" feelings, she began tentatively talking about anger. Referring to her tendency to "stuff" angry feelings, she said she stays calm by keeping the lid on but then loses control and just explodes like a volcano. After verbally exploding she doesn't stay angry, but feels safer if she pulls away, becoming guarded and withdrawn.

We also explored another important feeling. Because Susan didn't feel emotionally supported by other people, she often felt alone. When I inquired about where "alone" was located, Susan said that it was deep inside her chest, in the heart area. Following up on this information, I began asking "What's it like" questions. Susan gradually identified a small, empty, black hole – that's all that was there, a small empty black hole. As I continued asking questions, she said that the hole had tried to change its color by being bigger and nicer, "because who would value a small black hole that's empty?" Then she said "I'm stuck." When I inquired further, reiterating her words, adding "Is there anything else?" she explained that the hole was empty because no one could value a small empty black hole. The only other thing she could add was that the small empty black hole had been there almost constantly, for as long as she could remember.

In the following session Susan returned to the small empty black hole. She spoke of having put "the box of bad memories" away during her teenage years, hoping to put the past behind her. But she came to therapy because she needed to address the small empty black hole. And while black didn't mind being plain, the whole package wanted to be of some value. Yet, "only a miracle" could make *that* happen.

Susan's therapy had been moving until this point, but she started sinking into deep despair. She felt as if she had no friends, no support, and she complained that her husband wasn't meeting her emotional needs. She was crying frequently, feeling alone and needy. Her therapy entered the winter of her discontent.

While fall feels full of movement and activity, cold winds eventually take their toll and leaves descend to earth. These leaves cover the ground and protect it from the ravages of winter. As the therapeutic relationship provides a similar protective mantle, the important work of fall involves establishing a supportive, caring relationship – one that fosters growth as well as protects. The content of these sessions clarifies a client's difficulties, but important work happens between the lines of conversation. In addition to developing a relationship, we're adding material to the compost pile, helping it build, listening, watching, and waiting. We know that Winter is awaiting.

Winter

Winter is the season of hibernation. Energy dwindles, life slows down, and as the earth freezes over, rivers appear to stop flowing. Depression settles in, and even sunny days seem gloomy, for there is no green in sight. Green is hidden underground, beneath frozen surfaces.

While there is no movement on the surface of a garden, gardeners know that the core of the earth stays warm and life continues beneath its frozen crust. We continue preparing for spring. The earth may seem frozen, but we keep adding material to the compost pile. And when seed catalogues arrive, we begin perusing them, wondering which seeds might be suited to our particular gardens.

Each garden has its own growing conditions. One garden has clay soil, while another is more sandy. Some are in the sun and others in the shade. They may be on undulating hills, in valleys, or on flat terrain. Every garden is a unique personality, with its own inventory of dormant seeds.

Therapists stay tuned to each client's garden. While growth seems to be at a standstill during winter, things are happening beneath the surface. Knowing that the frost heaves of winter will bring dormant seeds to the surface, we wait for these seeds to appear. Because these seeds can't start growing until the ground begins to thaw, we may need to protect them through winter's coldest nights.

When Susan became increasingly despondent I knew she'd entered winter. She talked about feeling discouraged, depleted, and hopeless. While she had previously been able to do things for her family, she lost this energy and began withdrawing from them. Some of this pulling back was beneficial, for she was trying to say no to other people, particularly her children. However, she also didn't like herself and couldn't imagine why anyone would like her, let alone love her. She described being scared stiff to talk with anyone, feeling paralyzed, unable to move.

As Susan's despair deepened, she started feeling like running away and being alone. She complained of feeling like an outsider, regardless of who she was with. And while all her feelings were in one small little place, she also started saying things like "I don't want to sort them out any more, nothing helps . . . it hurts, hurts bad." She was crying every day and having trouble sleeping at night.

While clients are liable to become depressed during this phase of therapy, not everyone gets as depressed as Susan. Her lack of energy, difficulty sleeping, and suicidal ideation were incapacitating. She was severely clinically depressed. As medication can help alleviate the physiological aspects of depression, I considered referring her for a medication consultation.

Since most medication relieves symptoms without resolving the underlying issues, my usual inclination is to avoid recommending it. However, there are times when medication is useful. It helps temper a depression during winter, enabling clients to survive until their ground begins to thaw. In this respect, some clients are like tender plants that need protection from the bitter frost. As these plants require additional warmth in order to survive, gardeners either cover them with a blanket of mulch or bring them into a warmer environment. Medication serves a similar function when it's used to provide temporary warmth.

I referred Susan to a psychiatrist who specializes in psychotropic medication. After meeting with Susan, he agreed with my evaluation and prescribed an antidepressant medication, which she began to take. As I also believed that Susan's husband could help provide the warmer environment she appeared to need, I recommended that they schedule a few sessions with their minister to work on relationship issues.

Although it took a while for the medication to take effect, it did help alleviate the physiological component of Susan's deep depression. While Susan was still depressed, she was able to face life a little longer and give therapy a chance to heal her inner wounds. In addition, the couples sessions helped enlist her husband's emotional support. Susan used these sessions to focus on her music, explaining that music is her "connection with life," and asking her husband to encourage this interest.

Medication and couples work both act like space heaters. While their warmth is welcome, they usually don't have the power to turn winter into spring. Susan's soil remained frozen. She kept feeling "alone, separated, isolated, not attached to anyone . . . and worthless." These feelings continued haunting her. They weren't grounded in the present but rooted in her past. I knew that Susan needed to locate these roots before her earth would be able to thaw.

After discussing the importance of predisposing experiences, we began gently digging into Susan's past. We followed whatever feelings rose to the surface, for they let us know where her soil was soft, ready to give. By tracing her feelings to their origins, we gradually explored the roots of her difficulties.

Susan's feelings of self-worth were tied to performance, and she desperately wanted to accomplish something that would be valued by someone else. As we probed the origins of these feelings, she recalled trying to please her parents whose constant yelling and criticizing tore her apart. When she was in junior high school she assumed responsibility for the family's cooking and sewing. She remembered struggling to ensure that she did everything correctly so that her parents wouldn't be angry. But regardless of what she did, it was never good enough.

While Susan's orientation toward performance was rooted in the past, it pervaded her present life, including her attitude about music. Susan enjoyed listening to beautiful music, attending concerts, and playing both the piano and organ, but she had trouble valuing her musical endeavors because she would never become an accomplished musician. When she repeatedly brought up this issue in therapy, I emphasized the importance of how music made her feel. If she enjoyed listening to music and playing it, then the process was important, in and of itself, regardless of her ability to bring such pleasure to others.

As we continued with our explorations, Susan talked about growing up in a world of black and white; there were no shades of grey. She described herself as developing a "self-preserving focus." And while she now knew how to survive, she didn't know "how to repair," how to heal her inner wounds.

Hearing Susan talk about surviving, I suspected that she might be ready to talk about the abuse. Sometimes old wounds need to bleed before they can heal. Since all of Susan's energy had been focused on trying to prevent anticipated abuse, her wounds hadn't been given the opportunity to bleed. Talking about the abuse wouldn't heal Susan's scars, but it could validate her experience, enable her to move through it, and begin the healing process.

The next time Susan referred to the abuse I gently encouraged her to talk about it in more detail. Although the memories were painful, Susan spent the session talking about being beaten by her parents. When she heard "pull down your pants," she knew what to expect: "You got the paddle, the belt, or the hairbrush. In my family this was experienced as normal." Talking with me validated her experience of the abuse. It wasn't normal!

Deep-seated roots can rarely be yanked out of the ground. If force is applied, they tend to react by increasing their grip and holding on as tight as they can. Slow, gentle pulls are more effective in easing a root out of the earth. And while the root itself needs to let go, the ground must also release its grasp. If the soil is frozen, only a piece will be freed. Deeper parts of the root will remain trapped in frozen earth.

Susan's abuse had long been hidden underground. In discussing the abuse we weren't digging into soil to expose a root or trying to wrench roots out of frozen ground. Instead, we followed the trail of a root and warmed the earth around it. We worked with the soil, sifting through some of her early experiences, exposing rocks and stones that had been stunting her growth. When previously repressed feelings were aired, new light was cast on prior events and she could begin seeing them differently. This process helped Susan sense that life might exist beneath her frozen surface.

When Susan went to her next piano lesson, her teacher asked her to sing a piece of music. She knew what her teacher wanted because she could feel it "someplace inside," but she couldn't sing the music. Struggling with this dilemma produced a shift inside Susan. Although I had never used the word "metaphor" with her, she came into therapy announcing that she had a metaphor. The "black and white" theme of a recent session had developed into a "trash compactor."

When Susan couldn't sing she felt as if her feelings had been put into a trash compactor. The compacted trash was black and white, but she knew there were colors inside and that she was afraid to let the colors out. She recognized that compaction served a purpose; it kept her safe. The initial compression had come from her peers as well as her parents, for she had never been comfortable with other children. And while the compacted trash had tried to expand in the past, Susan was very afraid of other people's reactions. She had never felt safe and couldn't let it expand. Nevertheless, Susan now felt a glimmer of hope. She knew there were colors inside the trash: "It's got red in there."

I, too, was pleased to hear Susan talking about "trash" and "red." In contrast to the small empty black hole of earlier sessions, these images had potential. Because Susan described the red as wanting to come out, I knew life was stirring inside her frozen earth. It would take a while for her to move through winter, but her sense of "red" was a harbinger of spring.

Though there are bright days in winter when the sun shines, temperatures soar, and the earth begins to melt, these days are usually followed by another icy frost. As one season never moves directly into another, we expect these ripples. Therapists also understand that while one process may be taking place on the surface, something else can be happening below.

Susan immediately went from talking about red into what she termed her "wilderness time." She again felt detached from everything, apart. But something new was happening beneath the surface, for she was talking about feeling angry toward people, particularly her husband and children, who expected her to keep nurturing them. Feeling angry frightened her. On one occasion she woke up in the middle of the night hearing her father yelling at her for daring to think that she deserved something. After hearing his angry voice reminding her that she was worthless, Susan recalled that any time she mouthed off to her parents she was "crushed" for doing so and told she had no rights.

Although Susan continued struggling with feeling worthless and being devalued by her present family, music provided a way of tapping into other feelings. In discussing issues related to her forthcoming piano recital at church, Susan said, "I want to let some of the red out." When I inquired about what would need to happen for the red to come out, she talked about red being very afraid to come out. And while we'd been skirting around red for many months, this time Susan responded to my "where" questions. She answered that red was inside, in the middle, where it fits; "it's adjusted."

Having located red, I began inquiring about red's qualities. After saying that it was soft and pliable, Susan decided that there was now some space around trash and that there were different colors in it. However, none of the colors amounted to anything because none of them were big enough to be useful. In addition, every color had a major deficit that couldn't be fixed – which was why it was in the trash. When we ended the session, Susan was unable to name the other colors or describe them further than saying that perhaps they were "ribbons."

Susan came into our next session bringing a gift – a loaf of bread she'd baked. I am usually reticent to accept gifts from clients, but this one was asking to be taken and cherished. After explaining that her gesture had symbolic meaning, Susan began talking about the colors in "compacted trash." She said that they were small bright pretty colors that wanted attention. Only one, yellow, was big enough to be useful, and it baked bread. Susan identified two other colors: red was associated with music, green with accounting. She then told me that trash wanted to be valued, nurtured. And while the yellow ribbon had more potential, because it was the least unhappy, she didn't know how the trash could ever be valued. Even her religious beliefs were inadequate for this task, for she said, "Only God can take that trash and put it in the dump. Why doesn't God do that?"

When I graciously accepted Susan's bread, I shared my honest feelings about the importance of bread, its nutritional value and life-sustaining virtues. Pretense has no place in therapy and I would never have accepted the bread if I hadn't truly valued it.

Gifts are complicated issues. The clients most likely to bring us gifts are people, like Susan, who devote a great deal of energy to taking care of others but yearn to be given to themselves. They're likely to repeat this pattern in therapy by taking care of us in a variety of ways. It is part of the transference, and countertransference, relationship.

Although I was trained to interpret gifts and to never accept them, I've realized that refusing a gift can be devastating for some clients. The important issue is not one of following a rule, but of listening to clients, reading between their lines, and hearing the meaning behind the gift. The meaning can be discussed and addressed separately from the question of to accept the gift. More often than not, I'll accept the gift, but use the occasion to emphasize that I am here to help them and not vice versa. I've found that most of my clients hear this message early in therapy, which usually saves me from having to deal with the issue of gifts.

Susan's gift was part of her therapy – a metaphor. By allowing "compacted trash" to expand slightly she discovered more colors and let one come out. While I wanted to value "yellow," the negative aspects of "trash" were also yearning to be accepted. I knew that something else would need to happen with "trash" before Susan could feel better about herself.

Although Susan now knew that there were colors inside "trash," she was still stuck in the same fundamental predicament – struggling against her imperfections and looking outside herself for value. Quite predictably, the melting, or in this case expanding, that allowed "colors" to surface was followed by another deep freeze. Despair returned and Susan was again suicidal.

At times like these, our clients' helplessness can be contagious. All therapists, but especially beginners, are prone to feeling discouraged during winter. As the earth is frozen, not much can happen during this time. Our tools appear to bounce off unyielding ground. Clients feel stuck and so do we.

Gardeners similarly get cabin fever in winter. We feel cooped up, trapped, with no place to go. Each slight thaw is a welcome relief, bringing smiles to our faces and joy to our hearts. But when winter reasserts herself we scurry inside, huddle beside warm fires, and wait for spring.

Seasoned gardeners and therapists learn to trust the cycles. Having watched many seasons come and go, we know that each season gradually rolls in while another departs. And every season serves a purpose: It lays the groundwork for the next.

The successive freezing and thawing of late winter produce frost heaves that form potholes in pavement and devastate New England roads. Frost heaves occur when moist soil freezes. The ground erupts into small volcanoes of frozen earth.

Frost heaves push old roots out of the ground and create crevices in the soil. Seeds that have been hidden underground are also pushed to the surface. When spring arrives these seeds will germinate, bringing new life into the area. Some will grab hold of the earth and mend its cracks.

Metaphors behave like dormant seeds. They rise to the surface because clients are actively wrestling with their difficulties, struggling internally. When Susan's struggle with the "trash compactor" gave birth to "colors," her ground was still frozen and the metaphor couldn't develop any further. This seed for healing remained on her ground, waiting for conditions more conducive to growth. Meanwhile, the roots of old patterns stayed stuck in her earth.

Susan's conflict progressed into more frequent periods of thawing and freezing. She began describing a series of highs and lows as she was rocked by one frost heave after another. While her highs were characterized by feeling fully present, "connected," she also frequently felt "disconnected, apart, alone" and suicidal. Recognizing that her detachment served as a defense, she realized how long she'd been detached and how much she'd been detached from everything.

Music continued to be a major source of solace because Susan didn't feel detached when playing by herself. Appreciating the importance of music, she not only scheduled regular times for practicing both the piano and organ, but began protecting this time, guarding it against intrusions.

Even though there were now times when Susan was "feeling better," she couldn't trust it. She was still stuck protecting herself, surviving. When discussing her inability to trust good feelings, Susan recalled that her mother would be nice and then turn into a witch. This repetitive experience was still influencing her relationships. For example, after a Christmas celebration during which her present family let her know that they loved and appreciated her, she spoke about being afraid to take their love in. She was afraid that if her family were to truly know her, they would realize that her parents had been right.

Susan's emotions were swinging from one extreme to another. Although she experienced "high" times, she continued feeling that "there's no space for me to be a person." She struggled with other people's expectations of her, particularly their demands on her time. While she believed that she always had to meet everyone else's needs, she was also haunted by the sense that she could never do it right. She felt angry about this predicament, wrestling with it every day as she went about the business of taking care of her family.

The successive freezing and thawing had its effect. Frost heaves littered Susan's landscape. They not only brought dormant seeds in the forms of metaphors, old patterns were also uprooting. Susan came in one day and announced that she had decided to "throw the file away." The file contained all the parental injunctions, expectations, and criticisms that she'd grown up with, including the belief that she must never accept a compliment. Soon after throwing away this file she also started a diet. Susan's earth was no longer frozen.

Susan's ground was shifting. But winter wasn't over. It entered another phase, the period we call "Mud Season."

Mud Season

Mud season is a New England phenomenon. It marks the transition between winter and spring. While surface soil has softened, the earth beneath is still frozen solid. Any moisture on the surface has no place to go. Since water can't drain into the earth, it remains on the surface where it mixes with soil, creating gobs of mud.

Transitions are rarely smooth, and the transition from winter to spring is no exception. Fluctuating temperatures and shifting weather impact the earth. Temperatures hover around freezing. At times the earth freezes over; other times, it melts. The sky can be clear one day, cloudy the next. And while rain transforms the earth into a sticky gooey mess, a period of warm sunny days frequently follows. The ground dries, becoming firmer and steadier. The many combinations and permutations of rain, sun, and temperature can wreak havoc on the earth.

Mud season lasts until the earth totally defrosts. It's winter's last gasp – an unstable phase. Clients are on shaky ground. While their soil is softening, old patterns uprooting and new possibilities emerging, they also get stuck in muck.

When Susan threw away her file she immediately felt like a huge burden was gone. She felt "free." But her sense of relief was short-lived, because she still felt inadequate, particularly with her husband. She felt "bad" whenever she couldn't meet his needs. This feeling was expressed in one of her rare dreams. In this dream her husband became angry with her, furious, and then left. This poignant dream portrayed her fear of being abandoned and her sense of never knowing when someone would turn on her with rage.

Susan was grappling with the aftermath of having thrown out the original file. Her ground was no longer solid, firm, and frozen; it was becoming more fluid. As the turbulence reverberated throughout her psyche, dredging up old fears and giving form to some dreams, her moods started fluctuating, moving up and down. After riding forward on the crest of a high, her feelings would crash down, and then be pulled by a strong undertow until another wave of good feeling would pull her back up. Shaking herself free of parental expectations had left her facing a more basic question: "If not perfect, then what?"

Susan struggled with feelings of inadequacy. She felt damaged and defective. In the past she dealt with these feelings by aiming for perfection. Now that she was living without her old file, she faced the question of standards. As she struggled with this question I talked about the condition of being human, imperfect, and mortal. I encouraged her to embrace her humanness by accepting all parts of herself, including her flaws. Susan wanted to be open to this possibility but said, "I think I can lower the standards for myself, but what about other people?"

While Susan enjoyed preparing for her piano recital, she worried about whether she would do well. Afterwards she described it as a novel experience because no one said anything bad, and people seemed to enjoy her performance. But a few weeks later she fell apart while playing for a group of youngsters in a relatively non-threatening situation. She felt devastated by this experience, because "If I don't do well, I don't have value."

In the midst of many discussions about feeling worthless, Susan made another important decision. Although we had rarely focused on her weight, she brought up the idea of starting a diet. I am generally opposed to stringent diets, but Susan was enthusiastic about one particular plan. Rather than squelch her enthusiasm, I supported her efforts. She began a liquid diet – an appropriate choice for mud season.

Susan's new diet prompted some discussion of issues around food. She tended to eat when she was alone, for food was the only thing she could legitimately give to herself. When we talked about giving to herself in other ways, Susan described being nourished by music.

Susan was swamped by a morass of feelings. In many ways she was feeling better. She was making progress with the diet and enjoying her music. Although she continued wanting to please people, she was making time for herself and saying no to others. Yet she was haunted by feelings of worthlessness. She couldn't escape them. They globbed onto her and refused to let go.

Mud season is characterized by this quality of increasing entrenchment in the midst of movement. As soon as clients begin making real progress, they also become incredibly stuck. It is important to let them get stuck, to not try to dig them out of the holes they're in. They need to thrash around, wrestle with inner demons. Only then will their earth begin to shift.

Shortly after Susan had thrown out her file she agreed to do a duet with someone. After months of preparation this performance went poorly, at least according to her. She felt as if she wanted to die and wondered whether she could live with something that wasn't OK. Knowing that Susan needed to wrestle with this question, I encouraged her to delve deeper into it. It was her muck. She needed to sink into it, get totally stuck in it.

Susan immediately focused on her badness, stating that she always worked hard not to let the badness out. And although she usually succeeded in controlling this badness, she didn't deserve love because her badness was inside. All of her was bad.

Our next session began with Susan talking about how she can't take it in when her husband says "I love you." After recognizing that this difficulty was another facet of her larger predicament, she again focused on her badness, mentioning the catastrophic duet in which the badness had come out in her singing. When I asked Susan where "badness" was located, she described feeling very dissociated from it; it had to be kept hidden away. As I continued asking questions, Susan described a shell and then recognized her metaphor, the compacted trash.

Metaphorical questions can be very elucidating during mud season. They help clients address their unconscious processes, the substratum of their difficulties. Although I'd often used these questions with Susan, she had previously been unable to work directly with metaphors. The metaphorical shift from "black hole" to "compacted trash" took place at an unconscious level. She didn't know it was happening.

As Susan became more stuck in her mud, the metaphor of compacted trash took on added dimensions and she was able to describe it in more detail. After saying that it was grey, and cubical or rectangular, Susan focused on its tightness and density, its intensity and density. It was pushed together and dense because everything that had been put in there was totally unacceptable. It was an outer shell with trash in the middle.

As compacted trash was no longer black and white but grey, I knew that something had changed. Endeavoring to empower the compacted trash, I asked, "And so compacted trash is grey, and tight, and pushed together, and dense. It's an outer shell with trash in the middle. And what does compacted trash that's an outer shell with trash in the middle want to have happen?" Susan answered that compacted trash had no right to want anything and just felt hopeless. Although Susan's mud was beginning to shift, it wasn't yet ready to let go.

Susan's mother came to visit in the midst of our sessions addressing compacted trash. This visit was an opportunity to explore "compacted trash" from a different angle. It confirmed what Susan had been admitting to herself: her mother was always right, while Susan's feelings were always bad and wrong.

Soon after her mother's visit Susan reported that she'd been crying frequently and her feelings were more up and down than ever before. Describing herself as "not knowing who I am, or what I can trust" she said, "I'm grappling with this core issue of who am I?" Clarifying this statement further, she added, "I've always been trying to please. I can't do it anymore."

Susan found that it was easier to feel connected with herself during quiet, alone times, such as when she was playing music, walking, or meditating. She was yearning for quiet. And while she tried to schedule time to be by herself, it frequently conflicted with other people's expectations of her. Her internal struggle to value herself and her own needs was enacted with other people. It was played out around the issue of her alone time.

Although Susan had been learning how to say no to many people, including her children, she had difficulty doing this with her husband. She felt that he didn't hear her, and she wanted to learn to say no to him, but recognized how much of her identity was intertwined with his. As she looked to him for her value, she couldn't tolerate him being upset with her in any way.

While Susan's husband supported her interest in the piano and organ, he resented it when her time to be by herself interfered with their together time. As Susan was grappling with feelings of worthlessness, she felt very vulnerable and wanted to protect herself. She knew that she could prevent her husband's anger by doing what he wanted, but didn't want to continue paying the price of this old pattern. This dilemma kept appearing, in one form or another, throughout Susan's therapy. She was trapped inside this predicament.

Therapy sessions often seem to be going over the same ground. Similar themes keep surfacing, and we bob in, out, and around related issues. As the seasons progress, the issues shift slightly. They develop new meaning and their nuances are different. But while we address clients' issues, it is the soil around them that needs to change. The important shifts take place in the ground.

During mud season, clients are in the throes of their dilemmas—grappling with core issues, struggling internally, feeling conflicted and torn. Their tension comes from having opposites – conflicting forces – polarities pulling against each other inside the compost pile. This tension generates heat, fueling inner fires. And though ground doesn't soften overnight, earth begins to thaw.

As long as Susan's ground wasn't ready to go from winter to spring she remained in a quagmire, struggling inside herself, grappling with feelings of "I'm not good enough." While she was no longer suicidal, she had periods of being racked by tears. This usually happened when she was alone. She cried and cried. Although Susan had cried before, there was something new about these tears.

When Susan started therapy she seemed almost dead. She managed to survive the daily tasks of living, but was frozen inside. Her feelings were squelched, pushed aside, compacted. And though she cried, her tears were frozen, hidden inside. If water escaped through cracks in her frozen earth and dribbled down her cheeks, they were tears of quiet desperation and inner resignation.

Tears of mud season are tormented, wrenched from deep within. Pain is dredged up but also released. And while Susan felt stuck, she was actively grappling with her issues. This inner struggle generated heat, and real tears came as Susan's earth began to thaw.

These rivers of feeling flowing from her body contained memories of abuse.

Years of abuse had frozen Susan's earth. If Susan hadn't internalized the abuse it would have remained an external conflict between herself and her parents. However, by trying to prevent the abuse she internalized the conflict. She began suppressing her own feelings and blaming herself. This process was symbolized by Susan's metaphor of compacted trash.

Susan brought up "compacted trash" after being unable to visualize her heart during a quiet time meditation. As she felt detached, cold and empty, she wondered whether her heart was in the compacted trash. I invited Susan to explore the possibility by slowing my words, using my voice rhythmically, and saying, "So, take some time to get to know compacted trash, all its qualities, what it's like, whether heart is there, and whether there could be anything else." After a while Susan said that there could be a peach pit, an old peach pit, in compacted trash.

As Susan had previously loved gardening, she was familiar with the composting process. We speculated about whether something in the trash could compost and turn into earth. But Susan was frightened about what might happen if the peach pit began to grow. She was afraid it would become a defective tree. Talking about the tree, Susan added that it would never bear fruit; it was damaged inside.

Although I recognized that Susan's term, "damaged," referred to having being abused, I didn't make any interpretations. And I didn't tell Susan that this was the first time any of her metaphors showed potential for growth. Instead I left spaces of silence between us, allowing Susan to keep attending to the peach pit and tree. Occasionally I asked a question about the tree, wondering what could happen next, if there was anything else, and whether it was all right with the tree that it might never bear fruit.

We were still talking about the tree when Susan returned to her familiar theme; but this time it had a different twist. She wondered whether she could value something that had been damaged. "Does it have to be perfect?" Instead of assuming the worthlessness of the tree, Susan was considering the possibility of valuing it, even with defects. Her ground had softened. She was moving closer to spring.

When ground is frozen, compacted, our various psychological

techniques provide ways of facilitating the composting process. While the warmth of a therapeutic relationship can heat the surface of soil, composting imitates nature's way of regenerating earth. It is the key to inner healing.

As composting requires a variety of materials, an adequate mix of opposites, therapeutic comments and questions are geared toward remedying our clients' imbalances by encouraging the growth of their suppressed, repressed, or otherwise neglected qualities. This process creates tension, the dynamic tension of interacting polarities. And the tension between opposites generates heat – fueling fires of creativity that gradually turn old patterns into loose friable earth.

Old patterns begin to decay. And if clients keep adding material to the pile, their compost continues heating up. It's part of the organic process. Then, somehow, deep within, a spark of creativity takes a giant leap. It crosses the space, the dividing line. This spark is a seed, a new beginning. In Susan's case, it was a peach pit.

Metaphors are slow to germinate. They keep waiting for conditions that can support their growth. And when mud season readies to move into spring, the earth settles down, becoming calmer and steadier. Gardeners prepare for spring by applying compost to depleted soil. Therapists similarly add compost in the form of support and encouragement, but clients also need to be nourished by the life-supporting qualities of their own compost.

When Susan started therapy she had been trying to feed her inner earth with food. And while food provides proper nourishment for the body, it couldn't feed Susan's psyche, her soul. After shedding the extra pounds of old destructive patterns, Susan ended her diet. She had a new body and a new attitude. Even though her food preferences were different from those of her family, she was determined to take care of herself – to eat the way she liked to eat and not sacrifice herself for her family.

At the same time, Susan spoke about another process: "I'm rediscovering all the things that have been important to me – cooking, gardening, music." While these parts of herself had been stunted by years of abuse, they were also her compost, her fertilizer. These activities, as well as her spiritual practices, nourished her soul.

Through learning how to nourish herself, Susan began letting go of self-abusive patterns. And as she stopped compacting her inner earth, she found space for new feelings, new possibilities. She resumed growing.

When stunted plants begin to grow, they send roots deep into the soil below. These roots gently loosen soil, creating air spaces for other organisms. And as life returns to the earth, it becomes capable of supporting growth. It is ready for Spring.

Spring

Sap starts flowing and spring bursts forth – full of movement and activity. When green appears, the landscape becomes alive with color. And as green grows by leaps and bounds, a sense of speed and urgency permeates the air. The excitement affects everyone, but gardeners have a particularly hard time keeping up with spring chores. Everything happens at once.

Inside our offices, the slow hard work of winter is paying off. Dormant seeds germinate. As fertile soil is ready and waiting, clients surge ahead with spurts of growth. And while some clients describe feeling reborn, others use words like "whole" and "happy."

I knew that spring had finally arrived when Susan stopped talking about feeling fragile and started mentioning feeling good. After describing herself as feeling more free of the past and more connected with herself and God, Susan said, "Right now I just want to be who I am." She was also walking without listening to music, enjoying the process of being with herself.

Having recently bought herself a new wardrobe, Susan spoke about everything feeling new. The most important change was the one inside herself, but other people noticed the outward signs of her inner shifts. While many people congratulated her on her weight loss, some added that she also seemed more vibrant and alive. Even her clothes were more colorful than the ones she had worn before.

In speaking about the newness of losing weight and discovering herself, Susan began talking about difficulties she was having with her husband. While up until then she had been scared to do anything other than please him, she had started risking her husband's displeasure. In her words, "I'm fighting for what I've found. . . . I've made so many internal shifts. . . . It's not going to get knocked away."

Susan wanted to be able to tolerate her husband's anger. Realizing that she wasn't responsible for his angry feelings – they were his feelings, not hers – she spoke bravely about what would happen if she stopped protecting her husband from becoming angry: "Jim's anger will be his and he'll have to deal with it." But while Susan was able to see this intellectually, she felt scared whenever he was upset with her.

Susan's growth spurt was reflected in her dream life. She was remembering some of her dreams and, on one occasion, talked about wanting to go back to sleep to have it resolve. This particular dream involved three main figures, one female and two males. The woman was trying to find one of the men, a man she was engaged to marry. This man had been in prison but had escaped, even though he was due to be released soon for outstanding behavior. The woman was pleading with the authorities, asking them to help her find this man because she somehow knew that he wasn't under his own power. The man she was looking for was in a desert, being forced to work by a man with a gun. The prisoner's job was to turn the desert into a beautiful place. While he liked the work, he was being coerced to do it.

Since dreams contain important information about less conscious processes, I usually encourage clients to listen to their dreams by playing with the images and hearing their underlying messages. I may also offer my own associations to help enlarge upon their meaning, but I try to avoid imposing my interpretations. Brilliant interpretations can be used to feed a therapist's ego instead of the client's therapy.

As the dream felt important to Susan, we spent a whole session exploring its meaning. Susan immediately recognized that the man with the gun reminded her of both her father and her husband, but she then went on to talk about the issue of power: "Nobody in my family could have power without a gun. Yet I admire people who have power without a gun."

Susan's dream seemed to be talking about different kinds of power. At first Susan felt it was saying that there needed to be an inner marriage before the desert could get planted. This marriage would integrate her two sides of hierarchical power, represented by the aggressive man with the gun and the passive, escaped prisoner. But as we continued playing with the dream's images, Susan realized that the woman was essential. She represented Susan's feminine aspect, her power-to, another form of power. As the feminine also involves a process orientation, in contrast to the more goal-oriented masculine approach, this part of Susan would enjoy turning her desert into a beautiful place.

When working with dreams we blend different threads of meaning together, looking for a direction or an underlying message. This particular dream was anticipating an inner marriage. Susan was struggling to integrate different facets of herself. She was weaving the hierarchical, more masculine, type of power derived from her upbringing together with the neglected, horizontal, more feminine form of power. But even when threads of meaning tie into a theme, there is rarely only one way of viewing a dream. Since the impending marriage involved three main figures, Susan wondered whether her dream was also pointing her in a spiritual direction – toward the trinity of Father, Son, and Holy Spirit.

Dreams depict the inner landscape. In Susan's case, her land was a desert, waiting to be planted. The three dream figures were key ingredients in her process of turning the landscape into a beautiful place. And while she had not yet found a way to integrate the different aspects of herself, she was unconsciously working on this process.

The richness of Susan's dream indicated that her compost was working. Her soil was alive and fertile, with old patterns transforming into new ways of being. This inner metamorphosis was reflected in comments like, "I don't feel like black hole anymore . . . feel there's something else there now." And while the peach pit didn't grow into a tree, it did germinate into a new metaphor.

After thinking about possible metaphors – a rose bush, grape vine, or fruit tree – Susan decided that she was more comfortable with the rose bush. Then the rose bush developed a life of its own as Susan continued talking about it. She described its grafted stock in which the past grows from below, but she could decide what to do with it. And while all the things in her trash had been man-made, the rose bush was natural.

The metaphorical shift from "small black empty hole" to "rose bush" confirmed Susan's inner transformation. As her ground was no longer frozen, I planned to suggest that Susan consider going off her antidepressant medication. But she brought up the topic before I did. She felt that even though she was still running into difficulties, particularly around issues with her husband, she was handling them well and wondered what I thought about her discontinuing the medication.

After discussing Susan's present situation, we agreed that she appeared ready to stop taking the pills. However, I recommended that she first speak with her psychiatrist to find out whether there was a preferred way to withdraw from that particular medication.

Clients are often ambivalent about ceasing to take a medication. While they want to be free of mood-altering drugs, they don't trust the permanence of their inner shifts and are afraid of reverting to old ways of thinking and feeling. Therefore, I wasn't surprised to learn that Susan had felt both happy and scared after her conversation with the psychiatrist. Although she was pleased that we both supported her decision to discontinue the medication, she was afraid that her happiness might be taken away.

After deciding to stop taking the pills, Susan had an upsetting dream. The following day she was consumed by fear. The fear kept building until she felt incapacitated, paralyzed. Not knowing what else to do, Susan decided to pray. She had an image of being blocked; pipes blocked. In her prayer she appealed to "God, the Plumber," asking him to help her in her time of need. After a while, her channels opened and everything flowed.

Susan was amazed at how freeing it was to be able to create an image of what she was feeling. Recognizing that she'd learned how to facilitate her healing, she talked about the strength that came from her music and quiet time. She no longer felt empty, but had a sense of being whole, of feeling free and open.

Susan's sap was flowing, travelling through spaces that had been compacted, blocked, frozen. Now that Susan had some space inside herself she could enter that space – her healing place, a sacred space. Prayer was her way of moving inside this space.

The important work of therapy has been accomplished when clients become able to facilitate their healing. They are no longer dependent on a therapist to be their catalyst, for they have incorporated some aspect of the therapeutic process and are able to use it with themselves. No wonder Susan described feeling free – she now knew a way of tapping into her healing resources.

Instead of struggling for control, Susan yielded to a process. Rather than trying to prevent something bad from happening, she could create an image of what she wanted. She had a sense, an idea, a goal in mind. As she didn't know how to make it happen, she let it take place. And while this inner fertilization of masculine and feminine reminded me of Susan's dream, she experienced this process as her connection with God.

Many psychotherapists, myself included, were trained to avoid talking about religion with clients. While we recognize that people have religious beliefs, psychotherapy has tended to be a-religious. It is rooted in an analytical, scientific, and intellectual tradition that emphasizes division, specialization, separation between psyche and soma. While physicians specialize in the body, psychotherapists have left religion to the ministers and priests, and confined their attention to the mind.

The perpetual pendulum is now swinging toward a viewpoint that recognizes interconnection. We're talking about the "new physics" and a "chaos theory" which proposes that events reach into the universe by reverberating throughout a whole system, and from one smaller system into ever larger, more encompassing, systems. Closer to home, some psychotherapists are returning to the original meaning of psyche – *soul*. These so-called "new age therapists" are a diverse group of people. They come from different training disciplines and utilize a wide range of therapeutic techniques. Despite their differences, they have one thing in common, a belief in the connection between body, mind, and spirit.

Many new age therapies are either too simplistic or too esoteric for my liking, but they have helped me reexamine the assumptions I made about growth and healing. These complicated processes take place inside and outside of ourselves, connecting us with a larger universe, the world of nature. While I don't know if there is a divine order to this universe, I do know that clients' values and beliefs are essential to the healing process.

I believe that healing is a cooperative venture between all the various parts of ourselves. If someone is of a particular religious background, or spiritual orientation, these beliefs need to be not only respected but recognized as a resource for healing. In Susan's case, her belief in God was instrumental to her feeling whole, more complete. And while this shift didn't happen immediately after her dream, she did sense that the potential was there.

Susan gradually recognized that her growth wasn't temporary. Instead of telling me about feeling good, she was talking about remaining in a good place. She was feeling loved by God and said "I'm a child of God." I was tempted to point out the psychological significance of replacing abusive parents with a loving God, but this type of interpretation would not have been helpful. It would have discredited her experience.

Susan proceeded to tell me that she had spent many years yearning to be a child of God. This wish went back to at least high school and had been with her ever since. She even had some pencils made up with this statement: "I am a child of God." Although it had been eight years since she had purchased the pencils, she still had them and was now putting them to use. What was originally a wish became a key to her healing.

I am not suggesting that Susan and I spent our sessions discussing her religious beliefs. However, psychological issues enter other arenas, and when they do I explore them with clients. This applies to physiological processes as well as religion.

When Susan started feeling better psychologically, she also began taking better care of herself physically. She was not only eating food that nourished her body, but taking time to exercise by going for walks and working in the garden. In addition, she began attending to some health problems that had been troubling her for years. Although I'm careful not to step outside the limits of my knowledge, clients often discuss health-related issues with me. These discussions are part of their healing process.

Healing takes time. Once the ground has shifted it takes time for dormant seeds to germinate, set root, and flower. Susan and I discussed many issues during this time. Sometimes we spoke about difficulties with her children. When she began feeling less intimidated by them, our discussions turned to conflicts with her husband. And while these conversations fed her compost and contributed to her growth, her healing was inspired by the rose.

Susan's metaphor of a rose took on increasing significance. As the rose spoke to her on many levels, it became her symbol for healing. She focused on its perfection, its wholeness. The fact that roses have thorns also intrigued Susan, for thorns don't detract from a rose's beauty. Thorns are accepted as part of its picture.

Although no one session focused on the rose, this symbol kept appearing and reappearing in one form or another. On one occasion Susan talked about the importance of having received red roses from her husband. In the language of roses, they meant he loved her. When Christmas rolled around Susan decided to do something different for her annual Christmas letter. Instead of the customary chronology of recent events, she prepared a rose parable to share with her family's various friends and relatives. It was titled "Perfect as a Rose: A Modern Parable."

Susan's parable began, "For thousands of years, the rose has been considered to be the perfect flower." After providing a few historical tidbits, Susan defined perfection as wholeness and asked her readers to note that she had made no reference to concepts of "flawless, without fault, pure, thorough, correct in every detail." As I read her words my mind went back to Susan's agonized struggle with imperfection. She had definitely changed.

After describing the many varieties of this perfect rose, Susan asked, "Doesn't each one have the potential to be perfect (complete, whole) in its own unique way?" She then went on to consider their needs, pointing out that each kind of rose has its own unique requirements. Then, lest anyone miss the point, Susan translated her metaphor for the reader.

Susan wanted each person to see how the rose related to them. After saying "you are a rose," she asked the reader to consider his or her unique and characteristic bloom, type of flower, and requirements for space and rest. For example, she asked, "Do you do one thing exceptionally well (a large flower on a long stem, maybe), or lots of things pretty well (a cluster of flowers on a short stem)?" Toward the end of her parable Susan invited the reader to consider perfection. She said

> You are a person, capable of blooming, a living thing with needs. You are all of that, and more, combined in a way that gives you the potential for wholeness, for perfection. (Remember: No single rose has the best size, the best shape, the best growing habits, the best fragrance, the best color, the most

blooms, the least downtime, etc. – assuming, of course, that someone could define "the best." This is not the perfection being discussed! Rather, a rose is perfect in its entirety, at all times. In New England, a dormant rose in midwinter is doing exactly what it must do to flower the following June.)

While I haven't done justice to Susan's thoughtful exploration into the nature of a rose, suffice it to say that the parable traversed two pages of single-spaced prose. Writing the parable gave Susan an opportunity to integrate many of the feelings and ideas she'd been exploring in therapy. They came together in her metaphor of a rose.

Susan's fascination with the rose didn't end with her Christmas letter. Deciding to investigate the possibility of growing roses inside her home, she was well prepared when her husband inquired as to her wishes for Christmas. She asked for plant lights and rose plants. After getting his nod of approval she scurried from one place to another, joyfully buying equipment for her project.

Once roses were ensconced inside her home, Susan began ordering others for outside. She enjoyed planting the roses and watching them grow. Although I hadn't told Susan to bring more roses into her life, I definitely supported her ideas. I knew she was planting her internal desert. It was growing into "a beautiful place."

Spring is exciting – a time of heightened creativity and rapid growth. Watching clients grow is a joy for every therapist. It's what our work is about, what we hope for and strive toward. But the fast pace of spring takes a lot of energy. Growth gradually slows down and moves into the next phase – Summer.

Summer

The demanding pace of spring winds into summer's easy rhythm. Rays of sunshine brighten every nook and cranny, endowing the world with an aura of peace, tranquility, and well-being. Most of us enjoy being outside, where we float on soft breezes, feeling lulled by their warmth. Languid days and steamy nights contribute to the torpor that readily envelopes us all.

Having established their roots and unfurled their limbs, plants display their blossoms and begin bearing fruit. They concentrate on ripening. Gardeners might add a little water or apply some mulch, but our heavy work is finished. We continue watching over the plants, cultivating here and there, until it's time to gather the fruit that nature generously provides.

While therapists might be tempted to sit back and languish in the warm summer sun, there is still more work to be done. Clients have usually started to blossom but have yet to complete the spiral and move on with their lives. Even though therapy flows back and forth between internal issues and external relationships, most therapists tend to emphasize one orientation more than another. Once our clients start changing, these changes reverberate through all aspects of their lives. Therapy then shifts direction to complete the spiral.

In deciding whether to see a person for individual therapy instead of couple, family, or group therapy, I try to determine which modality, or combination, will be most effective for that client's particular problem. I recommend individual therapy if I believe that the difficulty is more internal, with roots leading to the past. My own style of individual therapy focuses on a person's inner life, their internal dynamics, their intrapsychic issues. Even though many sessions involve discussing current interpersonal situations, we also weave in and out between the interpersonal situation and its inner manifestation – the meaning it has for my client – its background, its history.

While change is taking place and internal dynamics are shifting, clients struggle to integrate the inner shifts with other parts of their lives. This weaving process is apparent during every phase of therapy, but it is the primary task of summer. While winter is spent more indoors, during summer we move outside and focus on interpersonal relationships.

When people change, their relationships with other people are often thrown off balance. This unbalanced situation is a marvelous opportunity for these relationships to grow. In Susan's case this natural sequence of events was exacerbated by an unexpected happening. Her husband lost his job.

After Susan rooted inside herself, she blossomed into a vibrant, alive, whole human being. Having also started branching out and connecting with other people, she was forming a few friendships and no longer felt quite as isolated or alone. But she was still encountering difficulty in her relationships with the people who were closest to her – her family. As she put it on different occasions, "I'm OK with myself, but not in any close relationships. . . . I like myself, but I don't feel appreciated by anyone I live with, or valued in the wider world."

Susan struggled with the question of how to be close to her husband and also remain true to herself. Because she had been a pleaser, their relationship had been structured around Jim's wishes and desires. Even without his asking, she molded herself to meet his needs. But when Susan began taking better care of herself, listening to her own feelings and desires, she started pursuing her own interests and activities, and began saying no to Jim.

Jim was accustomed to being Susan's top priority, and had difficulty adjusting to this shift. Then, in addition to this stress, he also lost his job. Feeling devastated, he escalated his demands for Susan's care and attention. This situation intensified Susan's conflict, for she cared about Jim and wanted to be of help to him but didn't want to sacrifice the many gains she'd made for herself. She felt unsettled, uprooted, whenever her husband tugged on her heartstrings.

As Susan had difficulty staying grounded inside herself while connecting with other people, I asked whether she might be interested in concretizing her metaphor of the rose. In my experience, it is often helpful for clients to incorporate their therapeutic metaphors into symbols, things that they can keep with them, such as a piece of jewelry or an item of clothing. This symbol behaves like an amulet – reinforcing certain feelings while warding against others.

Susan immediately produced the idea of buying a ring, a ring with a rose. Shortly after our discussion, she found two rings that appealed to her. Though the rings were quite different, they each had a rose motif. As she couldn't decide between them, she bought both. They inspired different feelings.

Susan began wearing one of her rose rings every day. She told me that there were times when she really needed the rings, for touching a ring, feeling it on her finger, gave her a feeling of wholeness. But while she was pleased that her symbol could elicit such feelings, she was still having trouble with her husband.

Although Susan recognized that Jim needed to work through some issues of his own, she had been accustomed to preventing problems and didn't know how to let him grapple with difficulties. When we discussed this issue, I spoke of allowing Jim to "stew in his own juices." While Susan liked this image and spoke of "turning up the heat," she initially didn't know how to do this. Instead, she continued resorting to her customary defense – distancing.

Susan wasn't considering divorce, but other clients have been tempted to solve their relationship issues this way. Some of them start therapy wondering whether they should remain married to their spouses. After clarifying their own issues and growing internally, the question of divorce may again rise to the surface.

Summer is the season when clients are tempted to weed certain people out of their lives. Instead of working through the problems in their relationships, they sever friendships that no longer seem satisfying, or consider divorce. Some therapists, and gardeners, encourage such behavior, but I have a different attitude toward weeding.

Many gardeners believe in the importance of weeding. They spend their summer days culling every intruder, without considering whether a "weed" is edible, or if it might contribute to the garden in some other way. I am more discriminating about weeding because I believe that as long as other plants aren't too close, thereby choking a particular plant out of existence, having plants nearby is beneficial. When plants are in close proximity to one another, they shade the soil and prevent expiration of moisture from the area. Other benefits of not weeding come from an organic gardening practice called companion planting.

Companion planting recognizes that plants interact with one another. In natural settings, plants that tend to grow in close proximity have generally been found to assist each other's growth. Although scientists are only beginning to discern the reasons for these mutual influences, companion planting traditions recognize that certain plant combinations are beneficial while others are detrimental.

I believe that intimate relationships provide similar companionship and mutual benefit. While toxic relationships do require weeding, it is often possible to work with a relationship and help it grow. Sometimes I refer a couple for therapy, or recommend family work, but in many situations, including Susan's, one or both people are not open to the idea. Under these circumstances I continue working with my client, helping him or her find a way of shifting the dynamics of the relationship.

Susan struggled with her feelings toward Jim. She had been stuffing her feelings, boxing herself in, not letting her emotions show, for so many years that she often had difficulty figuring out how she really felt about situations. When she took the time to sort through feelings, to identify what she was feeling and why, she began to realize how angry she was with Jim. And she actually *felt* angry.

Susan complained that Jim always put pressure on her. He knew what he wanted and pushed to get it. As she didn't know how to deal with his pressure, other than by giving in, she became angrier and angrier. She also felt that Jim wasn't truly there for her; he only heard her when she reached her limit and fell apart or became suicidal.

I encouraged Susan to feel entitled, to be more assertive, and to communicate her anger. But she was too scared. Instead, she blocked herself off from the feeling, dissociated from it. In doing so, she also cut herself off from her husband. Susan understood this connection, for she said, "When I block it off and don't express it, I'm blocking him off too." No wonder she felt alone and isolated.

My orchid cactus bloomed in the midst of these discussions about anger. Although there are always plants blooming in my office, this particular blossom caught her eye. Susan marvelled at the flower, admiring its large size and vibrant color. During another session, we addressed its other characteristics: it needs cold winter nights to set flower shoots, it flowers for a very short time, and, while not a particularly attractive plant for most of the year, it bursts forth with magnificent blooms.

A few weeks later, Susan mentioned that she had unsuccessfully tried to buy a plant like mine. This particular plant spoke to her, for she too generally felt worthless but hoped that something about her might eventually be valued by someone.

Although I was taught to never give presents to clients, every scientific principle has its exceptions. I listened to the wise woman, heeded good common sense, and made an exception. Offering to take a cutting of the orchid cactus, I asked Susan whether she would prefer one with red or pink blossoms. Susan stated that she would be delighted with either.

I took a few cuttings of a red orchid cactus, put them in soil, and waited to make sure that one had taken root. After the cutting was firmly established, I gave it to Susan as a reminder to begin letting some of her red out. Recalling her earlier comments about red wanting to come out (see pages 141 and 142), I explained that red often symbolizes anger.

As Susan became more aware of her anger, she started grappling with fear. She traced her fear back to early childhood. Remembering being scared as early as kindergarten, she said, "It's scary to realize how far back it goes . . . this incredible amount of fear." She described fear as "a taproot." It was in her core, with feeder roots in memory and imagination.

Up until now Susan had found solace in all her music. Music helped teach her to feel her feelings and flow through her fear. Yet as she tapped into her anger she became afraid of expressing her feelings and started having difficulty playing the piano. She wanted to play the piano but the organ felt safer; it required less expression.

The summer sun may shine, but clouds can hide it from view. Days can be gloomy, and heat oppressive. Likewise, Susan felt stifled by Jim. And she kept struggling with anger. She was more comfortable with the feeling, but had difficulty expressing it. Once again, depression set in.

When I first became a psychologist, I learned that depression was anger turned inward. In recent years, I've also seen the link between depression and shame. Susan's depression had both elements. The image of the rose had helped heal her shame. Now she needed to address her anger, and the fear that kept her from owning it and moving through it.

Susan realized that her fear had been conditioned by her parents and reinforced by peers. She said, "By junior high school I was operating behind thick walls built to protect me. Those people out there really hurt me. I was afraid to be me. But behind the fear, I yearn to be close, share."

Memories of the past started surfacing, especially after her brother came to visit with his family. Susan learned that her brother also struggled with depression and had been suicidal. He spoke with her about hating their parents. After one particular discussion, she cried all night as she recalled frequent dinner-time battles between her father and brother. During one of these fights she had watched her father attack her brother and throw him against a wall. She remembered pleading with her brother, asking him to stop provoking her father. She had been angry that he hadn't followed her advice.

Susan's fear served a purpose; it protected her from being abused like her brother. While she was yelled at, scolded, and hit with a brush, by never contradicting and by aiming to please, she managed to avoid her father's full wrath. Her survival tactic worked back then. But now it imprisoned her.

Susan felt trapped by her predicament. While she could see the connection between her depression and anger, she was afraid of anger. She didn't want to be hurt by others, but she also never wanted to hurt anyone else. Whenever possible, she'd been avoiding conflict.

Even though it was difficult, Susan began finding new ways of protecting herself. As she grew clearer about whose problems were whose, she started letting her husband stew in his juices. And where she had previously yielded to pressure and backed down at the least sign of resistance, she now tried sticking to her gut feelings, being clearer with Jim and refusing to let him push her into doing things she didn't want to do. I supported Susan's struggle to shift this pattern of her established relationships.

Change is never linear. Change proceeds in a spiral fashion. It moves ahead while also circling back. Susan still described feeling inadequate, unworthy, and unlovable, but she knew that she was "in a different place." Confronting her present situation recalled old feelings and memories. We moved back and forth between past and present. During one session Susan vividly recalled her father coming after her and how she had separated from her body. She saw how such early experiences had colored her relationships.

Psychotherapy spirals round and around, often seeming to cover the same old ground. For example, after Susan's mother came to visit we charted the sequence of her feelings, seeing quite clearly how her feeling of "I hate her," transformed into "I hate me." We also observed this dynamic in her relationship with her husband, seeing how readily her anger shifted into depression. It was necessary to trace this pattern over and over, in different situations and with different people. Meanwhile, I encouraged Susan to try sitting with her anger.

Susan continued focusing on her relationship with Jim. After learning she could hold her own ground, "keep him from pushing in on me," she began expressing her feelings. This meant not only sticking to her true feelings but communicating them to Jim. And by asserting how she felt, she started pushing back, tentatively at first, but with more force over time.

With inner shifts transforming into new ways of relating, Susan again described feeling up and down. Glorious interludes, filled with sunshine and warmth, were followed by dark, dreary days. At times, her summer felt endless. There were periods of draught. The atmosphere became charged and thunderstorms threatened; they felt frightening, but they cleared the air.

As summer progresses, storms abate. The air settles, grows cooler, and readies for Fall.

Evolution

A natural model of psychotherapy balances masculine with feminine, mind with body, and right brain with left. The role of the therapist is that of a gardener, blending the art of the wise woman with the discipline of the scientist. Gardeners use a variety of tools in helping people grow.

Growth is re-creation, creating the self over and over again. If this process is interrupted, the spiral becomes a self-perpetuating cycle, fixed in the same groove, stuck in muck. Therapy is the process of shifting relationships, reinstating the spiral, moving on.

Clients seek us out because they feel stuck. Instead of growing, they're grappling with a part of their selves, trying to control it, struggling to get rid of it. They're locked in battle. This adversarial relationship keeps them from growing, for they never consider the possibility that this part may have something to contribute, something to offer toward the whole.

Whenever we become locked in battle, fixed in adversarial relationships, we keep our selves from growing. This can happen outside as well as inside our selves. In order for change to take place the relationship needs to shift.

Change takes place in the undercurrents. It usually happens in small increments, gradual movements. Sometimes it builds into an explosion that rocks the bottom of one's being, a violent eruption from below. More often it's a shifting of tides – an opening where there was a wall, harmony where there were disparate conflicting parts, communication where there was disconnection. Regardless of how it happens, change is movement – going from a pool of stagnant standing water to a fresh flowing stream.

People want to change. Sometimes they turn to therapy expecting miraculous resolutions of their difficulties, looking for a solution to come from outside their selves, hoping their symptoms will disappear with the wave of a magic wand or vocalized incantation. However, one, two, or even three 50-minute sessions a week are mere drops of water in the ocean of their lives. Therapy is beneficial only in as much as it enters their internal process, activating their compost and becoming part of their nature.

The process of therapy follows a seasonal cycle. But like different areas of the country, each person has their own way of moving through the seasons. For example, one person's earth is more frozen than another's. And frozen earth, like Susan's, requires lengthier therapy.

Therapists provide an environment for growth. We help clients become familiar with the many facets of their inner selves, their apparent opposites – valuing each polarity, helping them balance each other, create harmony together. The direction for growth comes from within. It travels in a spiral, centering and connecting, moving out from the center in ever-widening circles. And when clients are freely flowing, sensing their inner tides, dancing in tune with their rhythms, the time comes to say goodbye.

In preparing clients to say goodbye, we usually review their therapy and talk about changes that have occurred. Clients talk about their internal shifts. While they know that they will miss therapy, they will be taking their therapy with them. It is now inside them. Our voices will go with them.

While therapists readily talk about clients identifying with us, incorporating us into their being, we have more difficulty acknowledging that our lives are touched by the people we see in our offices. Yet I know I am affected by clients and changed by our work. When they leave therapy a part of me moves on with them, and a part of them stays inside me. I'm pleased to see them moving on with their lives, but as they have usually earned a place in my heart, I am fond of them, care about them, and will miss them. Saying goodbye has a bittersweet taste.

Susan came in for her last session. After seating herself in the chair she began talking about driving up the driveway. While she had not thought about what she would talk about that day, the moment she turned into the driveway her head was filled with many associations. As she drove along she realized she would miss this drive – her pathway into another world, another space.

She took her time along the drive, looking around, seeing the sheep, chickens, fields, stream, and gardens. And as she walked up the path toward the door, she realized that she'd seen many seasons come and go.

We spoke of the seasons of her therapy. Her inner journey began during fall. She started shedding leaves, letting go, releasing the old to make room for the new. While her outward appearance initially turned bright, inner darkness was descending. She tried to get in touch with her inner nature, but first had to release the outward manifestations of her self.

Winter was her time of despair. She felt detached and empty, depleted and worthless. Her soil was compacted, frozen. But she explored the roots of her despair and began feeling angry. She re-membered abuse.

Yet she continued down the path, allowing it to lead her where she needed to go, shedding many tears on her frozen earth. Her music was her solace, her respite; it warmed her. Her temperature started moving, swaying then swinging, from warm to cold and high to low. This successive freezing and thawing brought dormant seeds to the surface, and old patterns uprooted. But just when her earth began to melt she became stuck, unable to move, trapped in the inner quagmire of quiet desperation – mud season. She was conflicted and torn.

Tension generated heat. It fueled her inner fires. And when she stopped compacting her inner earth she found space for creativity. Her compost started working.

During spring she sensed a vibration from deep within. Sap began to flow and she connected with nature, her nature. A new metaphor germinated. And as a rose sent roots inside her space, her inner desert grew into a beautiful place.

Growth slowed down in summer. Energy was channelled into nurturing fruit. In the glow of summer sun, she connected with people, nature, life – and she ripened.

Now it was time to say goodbye, to shed some other leaves. She can now flow with her seasons, her nature, her process. And there are seeds within her fruit. She is a whole human being – firmly planted in the soil of herself while branching out, connecting with other people.

Watching Susan walk through the door, I knew that she could

continue moving on with her life. Her problems weren't resolved but she, herself, had evolved. When she stopped compacting her inner earth she shifted the relationship she had with herself. As she had rooted inside where her compost was working, she would be able to continue growing.

Creating compost was the key to Susan's healing, but gardeners never actually make compost. By tending the garden, and adding material to the pile, we create an environment conducive to growth. Creative therapists use many tools and vary each tool according to the situation. The strength of our relationships and the power of words enable clients to cultivate the soil within their selves. The art of therapy lies in promoting the composting process.

Psychotherapy is a journey, but it isn't a direct path and it doesn't move in straight lines. It moves through time, winding in and out, and up and down, following associations and making connections. Clients travel in many dimensions – moving in one direction, then another. We navigate between conscious and less conscious processes: between past and present, inside and outside, right brain and left brain, masculine and feminine, mind and body. And as psychotherapy sails through the seasons of its year, our movement assumes a spiral shape.

Psychotherapy is a spiral. We engage with one client, travelling round and around until his or her process shifts. When he or she moves on with life, we move on to our next client. This process keeps repeating, weaving its spiral pattern through all of our lives. And each time a therapy comes to its close, I find myself contemplating the spiral of this work.

My work is a mere pebble cast into the sea of life. While I work with individuals, helping them improve their lives, I'm also concerned about larger issues, such as the widespread subjugation of people, continual warring between nations, and the abuse of our planet. There are times when I look at the small area of my work and bemoan its insignificance when there is so much to be done – so much hurt in the world, so much damage being wrought.

The main difficulty lies in the nature of our relationships – within ourselves, between ourselves, and with our environment. Psychotherapists are experts at tending to these difficulties. As gardeners, we can work in harmony with nature, helping people move from antagonistic relationships to cooperative ventures. We may only work with a few people, but as we cast individual pebbles into the vast sea of life we can hope their ripples eventually join with others and produce a surge of feeling that sweeps across this planet–a tidal wave spiralling toward peace and harmony not only within ourselves but between people, nations, and with the Earth.

Bibliography

Achterberg, J. (1990). *Woman as healer: A panoramic survey of the healing activities of women from prehistoric times to the present.* Boston: Shambhala.

Alonso, A. (1988, March). *Women and shame.* Paper presented at the meeting of the Women's Interest Group of the Massachusetts Psychological Association, Boston, MA.

Arieti, S. (1967). *The intrapsychic self: Feeling, cognition, and creativity in health and mental illness.* New York: Basic Books.

Bandler, R. & Grinder, J. (1975). *The structure of magic I: A book about language and therapy.* Palo Alto, CA: Science and Behavior Books.

Barker, P. N. (1985). *Using metaphors in psychotherapy.* New York: Brunner/Mazel.

Bateson, G. (1979). *Mind and nature: A necessary unity.* New York: Bantam.

Belenky, M. F., Clinchy, B. M., Goldberger, N. R., & Tarule, J. M. (1986). *Women's ways of knowing: The development of self, voice, and mind.* New York: Basic Books.

Benjamin, J. (1985). A desire of one's own: Psychoanalytic feminism and intersubjective space. *Working Paper #2.* Milwaukee, WI: Center for Twentieth Century Studies.

Benson, H. with Klipper, M. Z. (1975). *The relaxation response.* New York: Avon Books.

Berkeley Holistic Health Center (Bauman, E., Brint, A. I., Piper, L., & Wright, P. A., Eds.). (1978). *The holistic health handbook: A tool for attaining wholeness of body, mind, and spirit.* Berkeley, CA: And/Or Press.

Bernardez, T. (1987). Gender based countertransference of female therapists in the psychotherapy of women. *Women & Therapy: A Feminist Quarterly, 6*(1&2), 25-39.

Binswanger, L. (1968). *Being-in-the-world: Selected papers of*

Ludwig Binswanger (J. Needleman, Trans.). New York: Harper Torchbooks. (Original work published in 1963)

Birns, B. (1985). The mother-infant tie: Fifty years of theory, science and science fiction. *Work in Progress #21.* Wellesley, MA: Stone Center Working Papers Series.

Bohm, D. (1985). *Unfolding meaning: A weekend of dialogue with David Bohm.* New York: Ark/Routledge & Kegan Paul.

Borysenko, J. with Rothstein, L. (1987). *Minding the body, mending the mind.* New York: Bantam Books.

Borysenko, J. (1990). *Guilt is the teacher, love is the lesson: A book to heal you, heart and soul.* New York: Warner Books.

Boss, M. (1963). *Psychoanalysis and daseinsanalysis* (L. B. Lefebre, Trans.). New York: Basic Books.

Boston Women's Health Collective. (1976). *Our bodies, ourselves: A book by and for women* (2nd ed.). New York: Simon & Schuster.

Boston Women's Health Collective. (1984). *The new our bodies, ourselves.* New York: Touchstone/Simon & Schuster.

Braun, B. G. (1988a). The BASK model of dissociation. *Dissociation,* 1(1), 4-23.

Braun, B. G. (1988b). The BASK model of dissociation: Clinical applications. *Dissociation,* 1(2), 16-23.

Breuer, J. & Freud, S. (1966). On the theory of hysterical Attacks. In J. Strachey (Ed.)., *Standard edition of the complete psychological works of Sigmund Freud* (Vol. 1, pp. 151-154). London: Hogarth Press. (Original work published in 1892)

Brown, N. O. (1950). *Life against death: The psychoanalytical meaning of history.* New York: Vintage Books.

Brown, N. O. (1966). *Love's body.* New York: Vintage Books.

Brownmiller, S. (1975). *Against our will: Men, women and rape.* New York: Simon & Schuster.

Brownmiller, S. (1984). *Femininity.* New York: Fawcett Columbine.

Burnett, F. H. (1971). *The secret garden.* New York: Dell. (Original work published in 1911)

Cameron, A. (1981). *Daughters of copper woman.* Vancouver: Press Gang Publishers.

Campbell, J. (1980). Joseph Campbell on the great goddess. *Parabola: Myth and the Quest for Meaning, V*(4), 74-85.

Campbell, J. (1985). *The inner reaches of outer space: Metaphor as myth and as religion.* New York: Alfred Van Der Marck.

Capacchione, L. (1988). *The power of your other hand: A course in channeling the inner wisdom of the right brain.* North Hollywood, CA: Newcastle Publishing Co.

Cheek, D. B. & Le Cron, L. M. (1968). *Clinical hypnotherapy.* New York: Grune & Stratton.

Chernin, K. (1981). *The obsession: Reflections on the tyranny of slenderness.* New York: Harper & Row.

Chernin, K. (1985). *The hungry self: Women, eating & identity.* New York: Harper & Row.

Chodorow, N. (1978). *The reproduction of mothering: Psychoanalysis and the sociology of gender.* Berkeley: University of California Press.

Christ, C. P. & Plaskow, J. (Eds.). (1979). *Womanspirit rising: A feminist reader in religion.* San Francisco: Harper & Row.

Citrenbaum, C. M. & King, M. E. (1985). *Modern clinical hypnosis for habit control.* New York: W. W. Norton & Co.

Cogan, P. (1990). In the dark of the moon: A vision quest exploring Native American views of menstruation. *Psychological Perspectives, 22,* 94-101.

Cohn, C. (1987). Sex and death in the rational world of defense intellectuals. *Signs: Journal of Women in Culture and Society, 12,* 687-718.

Coward, R. (1985). *Female desires: How they are sought, bought and packaged.* New York: Grove Press.

Cushman, P. (1990). Why the self is empty: Toward a historically situated psychology. *American Psychologist, 45,* 599-611.

De Beauvoir, S. (1952). *The second sex* (E. M. Parshley, Trans. & Ed.). New York: Bantam Books.

Dinnerstein, D. (1976). *The mermaid and the minotaur: Sexual arrangements and human malaise.* New York: Harper & Row.

Donne, J. (1961). Meditation; Now this bell tolling softly for another, says to me: Thou must die. In H. C. Martin & R. M. Ohmann (Eds.), *Inquiry & expression: A college reader* (pp.

466-467). New York: Holt, Rinehart & Winston. (Original work published 1624)

Edelstein, M. G. (1928). *Trauma, trance, and transformation: A clinical guide to hypnotherapy.* New York: Bruner Mazel.

Ehrenreich, B. & English, D. (1979). *For her own good: 150 years of experts' advice to women.* New York: Anchor Books.

Eichenbaum, L. & Orbach, S. (1983). *Understanding women: A feminist psychoanalytic approach.* New York: Basic Books.

Fischer, L. R. (1987). *Linked lives: Adult daughters and their mothers.* New York: Harper & Row.

Franks, V. & Burtle, V. (Eds.). (1974). *Women in therapy: New psychotherapies for a changing society.* New York: Brunner/Mazel.

French, M. (1985). *Beyond power: On women, men, and morals.* New York: Ballantine Books.

Freud, S. (1952). *On dreams.* New York: W. W. Norton & Co. (Original work published in 1901)

Freud, S. (1957). The unconscious. In J. Strachey (Ed.), *Standard edition of the complete psychological works of Sigmund Freud* (Vol. 14, pp. 166-204). London: Hogarth Press. (Original work published in 1915)

Freud, S. (1961). *The interpretation of dreams.* New York: John Wiley & Sons. (Original work published in 1900)

Freud, S. (1962). Screen memories. In J. Strachey (Ed.), *Standard edition of the complete psychological works of Sigmund Freud* (Vol. 3, pp. 303-322). London: Hogarth Press. (Original work published in 1899)

Freud, S. (1965). *New introductory lectures on psychoanalysis.* New York: W. W. Norton & Co. (Original work published in 1933)

Freud, S. & Breuer, J. (1966). *Studies on hysteria.* New York: Avon Books. (Original work published in 1895)

Friedan, B. (1963). *The feminine mystique.* New York: Dell.

Fritz, R. (1989). *The path of least resistance: Learning to become the creative force in your own life* (rev. ed.). New York: Fawcett Columbine.

Fromm, E. (1951). *The forgotten language: An introduction to the understanding of dreams, fairy tales and myths.* New York: Grove Press.

Gallop, J. (1982). *The daughter's seduction: Feminism and psychoanalysis.* Ithaca, NY: Cornell University Press.

Gallop, J. (1985) *Reading Lacan.* Ithaca, NY: Cornell University Press.

Gardiner, J. K. (1987). Self-psychology as feminist theory. *Signs: Journal of Women in Culture and Society, 12,* 761-780.

Gilligan, C. (1982). *In a different voice: Psychological theory and women's development.* Cambridge: Harvard University Press.

Gimbutas, M. (1982). *The goddesses and gods of old Europe: Myths and cult images.* Berkeley: University of California Press.

Gimbutas, M. (1989). *The language of the goddess.* San Francisco: Harper & Row.

Gordon, D. (1978). *Therapeutic metaphors: Helping others through the looking glass.* Cupertino, CA: META Publications.

Gray, E. D. (Ed.). (1988). *Sacred dimensions of women's experience.* Wellesley, MA: Roundtable Press.

Greenberg, J. R. & Mitchell, S. A. (1983). *Object relations in psychoanalytic theory.* Cambridge: Harvard University Press.

Greer, G. (1971). *The female eunuch.* New York: McGraw-Hill.

Griffin, S. (1978). *Woman and nature: The roaring inside her.* New York: Harper & Row.

Griffin, S. (1981). *Pornography and silence: Culture's revenge against nature.* New York: Harper & Row.

Grinder, J. & Bandler, F. (1976). *The structure of magic II.* Palo Alto, CA: Science and Behavior Books.

Grinnell, G. (1987). Women, depression and the global folie: A new framework for therapists. *Women & Therapy: A Feminist Quarterly, 6*(1&2), 41-58.

Grove, D. (1987). Syllabus and workbook for *Resolving traumatic memories.* Edwardsville, IL: David Grove Seminars. (1-800-222-4533)

Grove, D. (1988). Syllabus and workbook for *Healing the wounded child within.* Edwardsville, IL: David Grove Seminars. (1-800-222-4533)

Grove, D. (1989a). Syllabus and workbook for *Metaphors to heal by.* Edwardsville, IL: David Grove Seminars. (1-800-222-4533).

Grove, D. (1989b). Syllabus and workbook for *Resolving feelings of anger, guilt and shame.* Edwardsville, IL: David Grove Seminars. (1-800-222-4533)

Grove, D. J. & Panzer, B. I. (1989). *Resolving traumatic memories: Metaphors and symbols in psychotherapy.* New York: Irvington.

Haddon, G. P. (1988). *Body metaphors: Releasing god-feminine in us all.* New York: Crossroad.

Haley, J. (1986). *Uncommon therapy: The psychiatric techniques of Milton H. Erickson, M.D.* New York: W. W. Norton.

Hare-Mustin, R. T. & Marecek, J. (1988). The meaning of difference: Gender theory, postmodernism, and psychology. *American Psychologist, 43,* 455-464.

Harrison, M. (1982). *Self-help for premenstrual syndrome: New and revised.* New York: Random House.

Herman, J. (1984). Sexual violence. *Work in Progress #8.* Wellesley, MA: Stone Center Working Papers Series.

Hillman, J. (1972). *The myth of analysis: Three essays in archetypal psychology.* New York: Harper Torchbooks.

Hirschmann, J. R. & Munter, C. H. (1988). *Overcoming overeating.* New York: Fawcett Columbine.

Hutchinson, M. G. (1985). *Transforming body image: Learning to love the body you have.* Freedom, CA: Crossing Press.

Jaynes, J. (1976). *The origins of consciousness in the breakdown of the bicameral mind.* Boston: Houghton Mifflin.

Johnson, S. (1987). *Going out of our minds: The metaphysics of liberation.* Freedom, CA: Crossing Press.

Jordan, J. V. (1991). The meaning of mutuality. In J. V. Jordan, A. G. Kaplan, J. B. Miller, I. P. Stiver, & J. L. Surrey, *Women's growth in connection: Writings from the Stone Center.* New York: Guilford.

Jordan, J. V., Kaplan, A. G., Miller, J. B., Stiver, I. P., & Surrey, J. L. (1991). *Women's growth in connection: Writings from the Stone Center.* New York: Guilford.

Jordan, J. V., Surrey, J. L., & Kaplan, A. G. (1991). Women and empathy: Implications for psychological development and psychotherapy. In J. V. Jordan, A. G. Kaplan, J. B. Miller, I. P. Stiver, & J. L. Surrey, *Women's growth in connection: Writings from the Stone Center.* New York: Guilford.

Kaplan, A. G. (1984a). The "self-in relation": Implications for depression in women. *Work in Progress #14.* Wellesley, MA: Stone Center Working Papers Series.

Kaplan, A. G. (1984b). Female or male psychotherapists for women: New formulations. *Work in Progress #5.* Wellesley, MA: Stone Center Working Papers Series.

Kaptchuk, T. J. (1983). *The web that has no weaver: Understanding Chinese medicine.* New York: Congdon & Weed.

Karen, R. (1992, February). Shame. *Atlantic Monthly,* pp. 40-70.

Kearney-Cooke, A. (1988). Group treatment of sexual abuse among women with eating disorders. *Women & Therapy, 7*(1), 5-21.

Keller, E. F. (1985). *Reflections on gender and science.* New Haven: Yale University Press.

Lacan, J. (1977). *Ecrits: A selection* (A. Sheridan, Trans.). New York: W. W. Norton.

Laidlaw, T. A., Malmo, C., & Associates. (1990). *Healing voices: Feminist approaches to therapy with women.* San Francisco: Jossey-Bass.

Lakoff, G. & Johnson, M. (1980). *Metaphors we live by.* Chicago: University of Chicago Press.

Lawrence, M. (Ed.). (1987). *Fed up and hungry: Women, oppression & food.* New York: Peter Bedrick Books.

Leonard, L. S. (1982). *The wounded woman: Healing the father-daughter relationship.* Boston: Shambhala.

Lerner, H. G. (1985). *The dance of anger: A woman's guide to changing the patterns of intimate relationships.* New York: Harper & Row.

Lettvin, M. (1980). *Maggie's woman's book: Her personal plan for health and fitness for women of every age.* Boston: Houghton Mifflin.

Levitan, A. A. & Johnson, J. M. (1986). The role of touch in healing and hypnotherapy. *American Journal of Clinical Hypnosis, 28,* 218-223.

Lewis, H. B. (1971). *Shame and guilt in neurosis.* New York: International Universities Press.

Liss-Levinson, N. (1988). Disorders of desire: Women, sex, and food. *Women & Therapy, 7*(2/3), 121-129.

Locke, S. & Colligan, D. (1986). *The healer within: The new medicine of mind and body.* New York: E. P. Dutton.

Lowe, C., Nechas, J. W., and the Eds. of *Prevention* magazine. (1983). *Whole body healing.* Emmaus, PA: Rodale Press.

Maccoby, E. E. (1990). Gender and relationships: A developmental account. *American Psychologist, 45,* 513-520.

Mariechild, D. (1981). *Mother wit: A guide to healing & psychic development* (rev. ed.). Freedom, CA: Crossing Press.

Merchant, C. (1980). *The death of nature: Women, ecology, and the scientific revolution.* San Francisco: Harper & Row.

Miller, J. B. (1976). *Toward a new psychology of women.* Boston: Beacon Press.

Miller, J. B. (1986). What do we mean by relationships? *Work in Progress #22.* Wellesley, MA: Stone Center Working Papers Series.

Miller, J. B. (1987a). Women and power. *Women & Therapy: A Feminist Quarterly, 6*(1&2), 1-24.

Miller, J. B. (1987b, April). Women's psychological development: Connections, disconnections, & violations. Paper presented at the symposium on *Learning from women: Theory & practice.* Boston.

Newhouse, N. R. (Ed.). (1986). *Hers: Through women's eyes.* New York: Harper & Row.

Norwood, V. L. (1987). The nature of knowing: Rachel Carson and the American environment. *Signs: Journal of Women in Culture and Society, 12,* 740-760.

Nye, A. (1987). Woman clothed with the sun: Julia Kristeva and the escape from/to language. *Signs: Journal of Women in Culture and Society, 12,* 664-686.

Orbach, S. (1978). *Fat is a feminist issue: A self-help guide for compulsive eaters.* New York: Berkley Books.

Orbach, S. (1982). *Fat is a feminist issue II: A program to conquer compulsive eating.* New York: Berkley Books.

Ornish, D. (1990). *Dean Ornish's program for reversing heart disease: The only system scientifically proven to reverse heart disease without drugs or surgery.* New York: Random House.

Parvati, J. (1978). *Hygieia: A woman's herbal.* Monroe, UT: Freestone.

Pelletier, K. R. (1977). *Mind as healer, mind as slayer: A holistic approach to preventing stress disorders.* New York: Delta/Dell.

Perera, S. B. (1981). *Descent to the goddess: A way of initiation for women.* Toronto: Inner City Books.

Person, E. S. (1980). Sexuality as the mainstay of identity: Psychoanalytic perspectives. *Signs: Journal of Women in Culture and Society, 5,* 605-630.

Plant, J. (Ed.). (1989). *Healing the wounds: The promise of ecofeminism.* Philadelphia: New Society Publishers.

Polivy, J. & Herman, C. P. (1985). Dieting and binging: A causal analysis. *American Psychologist, 40,* 193-201.

Prochaska, J. O., DiClemente, C. C., & Norcross, J. C. (1992). In search of how people change: Applications to addictive behaviors. *American Psychologist, 47,* 1102-1114.

Prozan, C. K. (1987). An integration of feminist and psychoanalytic theory. *Women & Therapy: A feminist Quarterly, 6*(1&2), 59-71.

Reich, T. (1948). *Listening with the third ear.* New York: Grove Press.

Rich, A. (1986). *Of woman born: Motherhood as experience and institution* (10th anniversary ed.). New York: W. W. Norton.

Richards, M. C. (1964). *Centering: In pottery, poetry, and the person.* Middletown, CT: Wesleyan University Press.

Riger, S. (1992). Epistemological debates, feminist voices: Science, social values, and the study of women. *American Psychologist, 47,* 730-740.

Roberts, S. C. (1992, May/June). Multiple realities: How MPD is shaking up our notions of the self, the body and even the origins of evil. *Common Boundary, 10*(3), 24-31.

Rosen, S. (Ed.). (1982). *My voice will go with you: The teaching tales of Milton H. Erickson, M.D.* New York: W. W. Norton.

Roth, G. (1984). *Breaking free from compulsive eating.* New York: Signet.

Sarton, M. (1973). *Journal of a solitude: The intimate diary of a year in the life of a creative woman.* New York: W. W. Norton.

Schaef, A. W. (1985). *Women's reality: An emerging female system in a white male society* (rev. ed.). San Francisco: Harper & Row.

Schreiber, F. R. (1973). *Sybil.* New York: Warner Books.

Shames, R. & Sterin, C. (1978). *Healing with mind power: Living and feeling the way you want to–through guided meditation and self-hypnosis.* Emmaus, PA: Rodale Press.

Shore, L. I. (1992a, January). Connection and caring in the movies. *MPA Quarterly.* p. 12.

Shore, L. I. (1992b, April). Facing the trauma of the holocaust through images and words. *MPA Quarterly.* p. 14.

Shore, L. I. (1992c). Female cycles. *Llewellyn's 1993 Moon Sign Book.* St. Paul, MN: Llewellyn.

Shore, L. I. (1992d). *Healing the feminine: Reclaiming woman's voice.* St. Paul, MN: Llewellyn.

Shuttle, P. & Redgrove, P. (1986). *The wise wound: The myths, realities, and meanings of menstruation.* New York: Grove Press.

Sichtermann, B. (1986). *Femininity: The politics of the personal* (J. Whitlam, Trans.; H. Geyer-Ryan, Ed.). Minneapolis: University of Minnesota Press.

Siegel, B. (1986). *Love, medicine & miracles: Lessons learned about self-healing from a surgeon's experience with exceptional patients.* New York: Harper & Row.

Silverman, D. K. (1987). What are little girls made of? *Psychoanalytic Psychology, 4,* 315-334.

Simonton, O. C., Matthews-Simonton, S., & Creighton, J. L. (1978). *Getting well again: A step-by-step, self-help guide to overcoming cancer for patients and their families.* New York: Bantam Books.

Singer, J. (1976). *Androgyny: Toward a new theory of sexuality.* Garden City, NY: Anchor Books.

Singer, J. L. (1988). Psychoanalytic theory in the context of contemporary psychology: The Helen Block Lewis memorial address. *Psychoanalytic Psychology, 5,* 95-125.

Spence, D. P. (1987). *The Freudian metaphor: Toward paradigm change in psychoanalysis.* New York: W. W. Norton.

Spyri, J. (1925). *Heidi* (S. Watkins, Trans.). New York: Grosset & Dunlap.

Starhawk. (1979). *The spiral dance: A rebirth of the ancient religion of the great goddess.* San Francisco: Harper & Row.

Starhawk. (1982). *Dreaming the dark: Magic, sex & politics.* Boston: Beacon Press.

Stein, D. (1990). *All women are healers: A comprehensive guide to natural healing.* Freedom, CA: Crossing Press.

Stimpson, C. R. & Person, E. S. (Eds.). (1980). *Women: Sex and sexuality.* Chicago: University of Chicago Press.

Stiver, I. P. (1991). The meaning of care: Reframing treatment models. In J. V. Jordan, A. G. Kaplan, J. B. Miller, I. P. Stiver, & J. L. Surrey, *Women's growth in connection: Writings from the Stone Center.* New York: Guilford.

Stone, M. (1976). *When god was a woman.* San Diego: Harvest/ Harcourt Brace Javanovich Books

Suleiman, S. R. (Ed.). (1985). *The female body in western culture: Contemporary perspectives.* Cambridge: Harvard University Press.

Sullivan, H. S. (1940). *Conceptions of modern psychiatry.* New York: W. W. Norton.

Sullivan, H. S. (1953). *The interpersonal theory of psychiatry.* New York: W. W. Norton.

Sullivan, H. S. (1954). *The psychiatric interview.* New York: W. W. Norton.

Swift, C. F. (1987). Women and violence: Breaking the connection. *Work in Progress #27.* Wellesley, MA: Stone Center Working Papers Series.

Synthesis, the realization of the self (Vol. 1, No. 1). (1974). Redwood City, CA: The Synthesis Press.

Synthesis, the realization of the self (Vol. 1, No. 2). (1975). Redwood City, CA: The Synthesis Press.

Synthesis, the realization of the self (Vol. 1, No. 3-4). (1977). Redwood City, CA: The Synthesis Press.

Thomas, S. & Tetrault, J. (1976). *Country women: A handbook for the new farmer.* Garden City, NY: Anchor Books.

Tierra, M. (1980). *The way of herbs: Simple remedies for health and healing.* Santa Cruz, CA: Unity Press.

Tompkins, P. & Bird, C. (1973). *The secret life of plants.* New York: Harper & Row.

Torem, M. S. (1986). Dissociative states presenting as an eating disorder. *American Journal of Clinical Hypnosis, 29,* 137-142.

Tronto, J. C. (1987). Beyond gender difference to a theory of care. *Signs: Journal of Women in Culture and Society, 12,* 644-663.

Van Der Kolk, B. A. & Saporta, J. (1991). The biological response to psychic trauma: Mechanisms and treatment of intrusion and numbing. *Anxiety Research, 4,* 199-212.

Verbrugge, L. M. & Steiner, R. P. (1985). Prescribing drugs to men and women. *Health Psychology, 4,* 79-98.

Walker, B. G. (1983). *The woman's encyclopedia of myths and secrets.* San Francisco: Harper & Row.

Walker, B. G. (1985). *The crone: Woman of age, wisdom, and power.* San Francisco: Harper & Row.

Walker, B. G. (1988). *The woman's dictionary of symbols and sacred objects.* San Francisco: Harper & Row.

Wallace, D. B. (1986). Secret gardens and other symbols of gender in literature. *Symbolic processes in the creation and interpretation of art works.* Symposium conducted at the meeting of the American Psychological Association, Washington, D.C.

Walsh, M.R. (Ed.). (1987). *The psychology of women: Ongoing debates.* New Haven: Yale University Press.

Washbourn, P. (1977). *Becoming woman: The quest for wholeness in female experience.* San Francisco: Harper & Row.

Watkins, H. H. *Non-hypnotic ego state therapy techniques.* Available from Helen Watkins, Counseling Center, University of Montana, Missoula, MT 59812.

Watkins, J. G. & Watkins, H. H. (1991). Hypnosis and ego-state therapy. In P. A. Keller & S. R. Heyman (Eds.), *Innovations in clinical practice: a source book, Vol. 10.* Sarasota, FL: Professional Resource Exchange, 23-37.

Watkins, J. G. (1992). *Hypnoanalytic techniques: The practice of clinical hypnosis, Vol. 2.* New York: Irvington.

Watzlawick, P. (Ed.). (1984). *The invented reality: How do we know what we believe we know? (Contributions to constructivism).* New York: W. W. Norton.

Wilber K. (Ed.). (1982). *The holographic paradigm and other paradoxes: Exploring the leading edge of science.* Boston: New Science Library/Shambhala.

Weed, S. S. (1989). *Healing wise: The wise woman herbal.* Woodstock, NY: Ash Tree Publishing.

Woodman, M. (1980). *The owl was a baker's daughter: Obesity, anorexia nervosa and the repressed feminine*. Toronto: Inner City Books.

Woodman, M. (1982). *Addiction to perfection: The still unravished bride*. Toronto: Inner City Books.

Woodman, M. (1985). *The pregnant virgin: A process of psychological transformation*. Toronto: Inner City Books.

Women's Bodies. *Woman of Power: A Magazine of Feminism, Spirituality, and Politics*. Issue 18. Fall, 1990.

Index